Your Robe of
Righteousness

Dr. Sandra G. Kennedy

YOUR ROBE OF RIGHTEOUSNESS
©Copyright 2004, 2010
Dr. Sandra G. Kennedy

ISBN: 0-9740880-5-6

Published by

LIFEBRIDGE
B O O K S
P.O. BOX 49428
CHARLOTTE, NC 28277

Printed in the United States of America.

DEDICATION

To my Church family, Whole Life Ministries,
for your love and enthusiasm and response to
the Word of God;

To Charlene Kiraly, who labored tirelessly
to bring the spoken Word to the printed page;

To Pat Fitzgerald, my dear friend and co-worker,
who had the vision to share the Word with countless
others and who worked behind the scenes to make
it a reality, I am eternally indebted.

FOREWORD

*Y*ou are holding a book brimming with life-giving truth! This is not in your hands by accident, and I urge you not to let go of it until you have a firm grasp on the freedom it can bring to your life.

Dr. Sandra Kennedy has a deep-rooted revelation of God's power and love. The mark of that revelation sparks deeper faith and renewed confidence, joy, and hope in the hearts of others.

YOUR ROBE OF RIGHTEOUSNESS is a compelling teaching that unfolds Jesus' greatest gift—God's nature within us. The authority of the promises of God will overtake you as you read this riveting book.

Find the enduring victory you desire as you shake off the "old" and wrap yourself securely in a "new" garment - your robe of righteousness!

– Marilyn Hickey

CONTENTS

PREFACE

*A*t conversion God gives the Holy Spirit to live within us, but then we have something to do. We have to set our wills to bring a change within us, such as our entire nature and lifestyle. We must become dedicated to one purpose – to be what God wants us to be and to do what He wants us to do. That is to be committed to change. This is the purpose of the new birth. It's no good responding with enthusiasm for a month or two then giving up. The Bible says, *"...Let not Him that girdeth on his harness boast himself as he that putteth it off"* (1 Kings 20:11 KJV). In other words, it's not the one who starts, but the one who finishes that has the right to boast!

This is often the trouble with many newborn Christians. At the beginning they are full of enthusiasm and excitement, then when the pressures of life arrive we find them disturbed, depressed or "weary in well-doing." What happened? They have never allowed God who is inside them to deal with their heart and mind so as to ultimately bring them conformity with the image of Christ. Consistency is what God is looking for.

This book, *YOUR ROBE OF RIGHTEOUSNESS*, written by Dr. Sandra Kennedy, is most significant for this time, skillfully laying out the steps of righteousness that each Christian will take as they are led by the Holy Spirit – so that all believers will be transformed into "The Image of His Dear Son."

In all of my professional life of 56 years in the ministry I have never found teaching with such clarity, continuity and conciseness as this book. It has been written so that all who read will understand what righteousness is—how to be clothed with it and what is to be done by each believer to enter into God's glorious redemptive state in all of its fullness.

My earnest prayer is that multitudes of Christians will sincerely read this wonderful work of grace—and that they will experientially and willingly enter into this unique and marvelous gift God has given to His children.

– Dr. David Schoch, D.D.

*J*NTRODUCTION

J am thrilled you are reading this book—and believe what you are about to receive will have a dynamic impact on your walk with Christ.

Our God is so wonderful! We truly are a blessed people to live in this day and hour when God is pouring out His Spirit upon all flesh and a deeper revelation of His Word is awakening His people.

This is the Church's finest hour! She is beginning to arise and shake herself of the debris that has kept her in bondage and defeat—and is finally beginning to take her place. Transformed by the power of God's Word, this Body is being fitly joined together, as God has desired and planned from before the foundation of the world. She is becoming the brightness of His glory—a walking, mobile Temple—full of the power of God—each member a living fragment of the Bread of Life! What a time to be alive and serving this awesome God!

God's greatest gift to us through Jesus, our Lord, is righteousness:

- Through righteousness, we can have an audience with Almighty God.
- Through righteousness, we can be healed or partake of any of the exceeding great and precious promises given to us throughout His Word.

Our new birth into this Loving Family is just the

beginning; it is only the first step of a fabulous journey into the divine nature of God.

On the whole, righteousness has never been understood by the Church world. As you read these pages, it is my earnest prayer He will speak to you—and your heart will be so enlightened by the goodness of our God—that your life is forever changed!

– Dr. Sandra G. Kennedy

CHAPTER 1

THE GREATEST GIFT

*C*an you imagine what it would be like to be named king or queen of a nation? Residing in a majestic palace, with the eyes of the world watching, a crown is placed on your head and a regal robe is draped across your shoulders.

Suddenly, you are royalty!

My friend, what you are about to read holds the key to a future that far surpasses any earthly coronation. As a child of the King you have already inherited everything the Father owns – and have been given a Robe of Righteousness.

> *For God so loved the world that He gave*
> *His only begotten Son, that whoever believes in*
> *Him should not perish but have everlasting life.*
> JOHN 3:16

What an incredible love that we should be called the children of God!—that Almighty God, the Creator of the Universe, would reconcile sinful man to Himself by sending His Son in the likeness of man as our needed Savior. We can hardly fathom the depths of His love—what a price He paid to deliver us from the authority of darkness—how much weighed in the balance while Jesus hung on the Cross and shed His Blood. And it was just for us! Oh, the depths of His love are beyond mortal comprehension.

THE GREAT TRANSFORMATION

Eternal life is no small thing, but most of the Church world has no earthly idea of what that life has done for them or who they are in Christ Jesus. They have no understanding, not only of what occurred in them at the moment of their new birth, but about their rights and privileges of belonging to the family of God.

Most believers are unaware of God's standards of conduct and how they are supposed to live. But, if we are born again, we have undergone a complete transformation in our spirit; we are not the same person. At that moment God imparts all we need to overcome every adverse circumstance of life by giving us Himself. He puts Himself within us—eternal life.

That life initially moved us into the Kingdom of God, but it also continues to thrust us toward holiness and further victory as we learn to walk in Him.

AN ADOPTION PLAN

Eternal life is much more than simply living forever. In it, we receive the nature of God Himself. We move into the very substance of God; into His family. We are literally born of God!

The Father so loved us and was so excited to receive sinful man back to Himself and establish us in victory, that He didn't just save us, but opened up an adoption plan to make us an integral part of His household. As His sons and daughters, He has given us the godly legal right to become heirs to the wonderful inheritance He has prepared from before the foundation of the world.

Scripture states that it is our Father's good pleasure to give us the Kingdom! It's not something we have to beg and plead for. He earnestly desires His people to walk as the head and not the tail—to be *more* than conquerors over the kingdom of darkness. His heart's desire is for us to allow Him to activate the authority of Jesus in our lives—to go higher to a new dimension, to accomplish His will on this earth, and to be exceptionally blessed in its fulfillment.

> *Therefore, if anyone is in Christ, he is a new creation; old things have passed away; behold, all things have become new.*
>
> 2 CORINTHIANS 5:17

When we are born again, at that very moment, God makes us a new creature in Christ Jesus. Our sins are not just covered by the Blood of Jesus, they are remitted, completely obliterated by the power of that Blood and we are cleansed. He puts His very nature inside of us to raise us up to the God level—to enable us to sit with Him in heavenly places, not as servants, but as sons or daughters.

He puts His very nature inside of us to raise us up to the God level.

I am not calling us "God." I am simply saying that when He deposits His nature, His abilities, His Spirit, His love and power in us, we now have an open invitation to come boldly to the Throne of Grace in audience with Almighty God. We can have fellowship with Him. We can now commune with Him spirit to Spirit. That was a major part of His plan from the beginning.

11

MONUMENTAL CHANGES

When God created man, he was magnificent! This creature was made in God's image, in His exact likeness. Scripture states that man was wonderfully made (Psalm 139:14). He was perfect—just like his Father.

At that time, the Kingdom of God was within man. Adam and Eve had the divine glory of the Creator residing within those bodies of clay. They daily walked with Him and operated in His wisdom. God had breathed His own life into them. Indeed, His creation was outstanding!

But God foreknew that man was going to sin and fall prey under the dominion of the enemy, Satan. When that occurred, it was no trivial matter. There were monumental and cataclysmic changes that even reached the instruments of worship in the heavenly Holy of Holies.

In a moment, these glorious creatures became nothing more than an empty shell of what they had been initially created to be. Mankind was now separated from God by that sin and His glory had to depart from them. They no longer could walk with God in the cool of the day but ran and hid from Him out of fear.

THE RESTORATION!

The Good News is that before the foundation of the world, Scripture states that The Lamb of God was already slain (Revelation13:8)! The Word of God, Jesus of Nazareth —the Son of God—*tabernacled* among us. He was already predestined to come and redeem us from that dark kingdom and restore us back to the original Garden of Eden state. That was Messiah's purpose.

God created man to be just like Himself, full of life, having His very nature, simply because that is the way God desired man to be! The Father wanted man on His level, and God's will has not changed throughout the generations.

When we are born again and accept this gift of eternal life, God's glory—His indwelling presence—is restored within man again, one by one.

When we accept Jesus as Lord and Savior, the Kingdom of God is no longer without, but once again, deep within these bodies of clay as at the beginning. See, the infusion of eternal life, God's nature imparted into each of us, is all in the plan the Father had in His heart from creation. He desires man and earth to be restored to Himself and back to what He initially designed them to be! And in the end it will be just that way. In fact, God encourages us to move from glory to glory, higher and higher, toward that end.

TURN THE KEY

Although God has accomplished these glorious things in us, we must learn to flow in this new life. We must discover that we are literally delivered out of the authority of darkness and translated into the Kingdom of God's Dear Son (Colossians 1:13). Darkness no longer has any authority over us. That thought is overwhelming to most of the Church. Yet, God is not a man that He should lie—He does not say anything He doesn't mean or does not intend to fulfill.

Darkness no longer has any authority over us.

Since His Word says He has delivered us, that should settle the issue; we are delivered. You may be thinking, "If Satan's kingdom has no authority over me, how is he able to harass me so much?"

It's basically because we don't know enough about this eternal life and what it has accomplished for us. The truth is: *life always overcomes death, but life has to be enforced for death to bow its knee.*

We must take hold of *who* we are if we want this astonishing life to work for us. No matter what wonderful things God has imparted, He left it up to us to activate them. He did the work; the provision is accessible— and we turn the key to initiate what He has already fulfilled for you and me.

> *Life always overcomes death, but life has to be enforced for death to bow its knee.*

It is by faith we step out and reach for higher levels. Faith is simply trusting God that He did what He *said* He did. It is believing that He'll do just what He *declared* He would do, because it is written down for us in His Word. God cannot lie. If He said it, He will do it!

> *God is not a man, that He should lie, nor a son of man, that He should repent. Has He said, and will He not do? Or has He spoken, and will He not make it good?*
> NUMBERS 23:19

> *Paul, a bondservant of God and an apostle of Jesus Christ, according to the faith of God's elect and the acknowledgment of the truth which accords with godliness, in hope of eternal life which God, who cannot lie, promised before time began. [italics mine]*
> TITUS 1:1-2

God declares that His glory is back inside of the born again saints—He says that His nature is once again resident within us. It's God's nature in us that shows forth His glory, and the manifestations of the Holy Spirit begin to make themselves real in our lives.

FROM THE INSIDE OUT

Sad to say, in most of us, His nature is lying dormant because we have so many things to deal with in order to move into His nature—and yet we must. If we really believe that God's eternal life, His very nature, dwells in our innermost man, we will be ruled from the inside out. Our lives will be transformed by turning loose of the world, taking hold of our rightful place —our heavenly home—and seeing life from that perspective.

We need to learn who we are, see how the devil has tricked us, and discover why our faith is not effective. We think we've done everything we are supposed to do, but it appears that

When we ask Christ into our lives, eternal life, the very life of God, is implanted into each of us.

some things are not working and we wonder why. But once we understand righteousness, we will be raised from glory to glory.

If there has ever been a time to move out and believe those things that God says about us, it is now!

For the wages of sin is death, but the gift of God is eternal life in Christ Jesus our Lord.
ROMANS 6:23

The gift God has given us is called eternal life and is wrapped up in *"The Gift"* named Jesus. So when we ask Christ into our lives, eternal life, the very life of God, is implanted into each of us. In Him we live and move and have our being because He now abides within us. The more conscious we are of that truth, the more the reality of God will be exemplified in our lives and conduct.

BOLD AS A LION!

It's not enough to know a great deal of head knowledge about God; it is what we do with what we know that brings us victory. The extent of God's life we walk in is up to us—not Him.

Fight the good fight of faith, lay hold on eternal life, to which you were also called and have confessed the good confession in the presence of many witnesses.
I TIMOTHY 6:12

It takes faith to latch on to what the Father has given—to believe that we possess what God has declared. The Lord doesn't do this all by Himself. It takes us trusting God—believing Him—being bold as a lion—separating ourselves from those around us—and stepping out.

Eternal life is not based on feelings or a consciousness that we possess it. Nor does it begin the moment our body dies—but when we receive Jesus Christ as our Lord and Savior.

Think about it! If we are not already infused with this eternal life the moment we pass from this earthly existence, we are not going to heaven. Eternal life is what takes the sting of death away.

Sadly, most of us are more tuned to who we are in the natural than who we are in the spirit realm. We are so focused on our surroundings that it is difficult to move into what God has prepared for us from the beginning.

TWO OPPOSING REALMS

We tend to think of and measure our life in the context of natural things. For example, we see ourselves as a wife or husband, having two children, working at a particular company, this many years old, having a certain college degree.

These details are simply our natural identity. God thinks of us totally differently. But if in our minds this human identity overrules what God says we are in His Word, we are not growing in the things of God.

If how we view ourselves, based on our natural circumstances, is more real to us than what God says, we are in error. For instance, if our body is plagued with sickness and disease and we see ourselves sick, we are in opposition to God because He declares that we are healed. Who we are in the spirit realm must take precedence over who we are in the natural realm or we won't have victory.

Who we are in the spirit realm must take precedence over who we are in the natural realm or we won't have victory.

SHAKING FREE!

What the Word of God says about us must be the final authority. Remember, the Father is trying to do a tremendous thing in our lives. He is waiting for His sons and daughters to manifest themselves and shine forth with the blessings He has already purchased.

For whatever is born of God overcomes the world. And this is the victory that has overcome the world—our faith.

1 JOHN 5:4

17

From God's point of view, we are already conquerors, even when circumstances seem contrary. From His perspective, we have moved into eternal life and have the privileges of such. But it takes faith in what God has said about us to attain victory.

The Almighty is looking for us to *believe* what He said and then to *act* upon it. Once again, we must settle the issue that God is not a liar.

Without doubt this takes going totally and completely against our natural man—because natural man does not live for God. The present world, with its temptations and enticements, tries to seize and pull us to itself. Yet we must be in the process of shaking ourselves free from its clutches in order to move to a higher level of life. Again, that process rests in our hands, not His.

JUST DO IT!

When God bestowed eternal life into us, He connected us to all of the resources of heaven through the Word of God. But if we do not believe the Word enough to act on it, it has no value to us.

To know the Word and not *do* it, turns into a curse. At some point, we must demonstrate what we *know* to do in order to clean up everything around us and reach the next level. We can't leap from one plateau of glory to the next with this baggage hanging around our neck.

How far we go with God is not determined by how smart we are—or how much Bible we know. It is based totally on what we decide to believe in His Word and whether we choose to step out of our old patterns and make the necessary changes. The question is: How much of God do we want? How much victory do we desire? If we are willing to pay the price of letting His life explode in us, we will have the ability to move on and gain the victory for which we have prayed.

In reality, we are God's sons and daughters who have been endowed with a fabulous inheritance. We are well on our way to the restoration God designed from the beginning —and the promise of being conformed to the image of God's Son, Jesus, our King!

Eternal life has set us on this heavenly pathway of victory! What a mighty God we serve—He is so wonderful!

Now let's find out from Scripture what enables Him to bless a sinful people with this gift of eternal life.

CHAPTER 2

*Y*OU'RE JUSTIFIED!

*T*he fall of man did not catch God by surprise nor catch Him off guard. Before the foundation of the world, there was a plan established to restore mankind back to Himself in his full glory!

All who dwell on the earth [in tribulation] will worship him [the antichrist], whose names have not been written in the Book of Life of the Lamb slain from the foundation of the world. [italics and inserts mine]
REVELATION 13:8

There was nothing that required God to reconcile His creation—nothing demanded that He redeem them from the kingdom of darkness. He was quite aware that man would spurn and mock Him, even shake his fist in hatred toward heaven, and blast Him with the words of his mouth.

Yet, the intense love within Jehovah compelled Him—drove Him in compassion to reach out for His man in fellowship and restoration—even before he was created.

Therefore, just as through one man sin entered

> *the world, and death through sin, and thus death
> spread to all men, because all sinned—*
>
> ROMANS 5:12

Sin now separated them, and death—not life—dwelt within the hearts of men. Man was sinful, but even God in His compassion and grace could not overlook the sin that was committed. No matter how merciful He is, He could not wipe it clean, for God is holy and righteous.

This scripture states that by one man's transgression, sin had entered into the world and death came because of that iniquity. Through this one man, death passed to all men down through the generations.

IS THERE HOPE?

No individual born through the sands of time escaped this "death seed" within his bosom; every man entered into captivity and bondage without recourse. We could not even approach this Holy God because of the sin we had become. We had a debt we could never pay; locked up in darkness without hope of escape.

We had a debt we could never pay, locked up in darkness without hope of escape.

> *In the beginning was the Word, and the Word
> was with God, and the Word was God. He was in the
> beginning with God. And the Word became flesh and dwelt
> among us, and we beheld His glory, the glory as of the
> only begotten of the Father, full of grace and truth.*
>
> JOHN 1:1-2,14

> *Inasmuch then as the children have partaken of flesh*

21

and blood, He Himself likewise shared in the same, that
through death He might destroy him who had the power of death,
that is, the devil, and release those who through fear
of death were all their lifetime subject to bondage.

HEBREWS 2:14-15

God had a plan. It was foreordained that He would come to us—and become one of us. Because we could never come to Him, He abounded toward you and me. This *Sent One*, called the Redeemer, would carry the sinless, spotless Blood of God within His veins and willingly pour it out for the redemption of mankind.

At the right time, Jesus, the Word of the Living God, born by Mary, but Fathered by the Almighty, came to earth and lived among men. He was anointed of God in the River Jordan to go about doing good and healing all that were oppressed of the devil (Acts 10:38)—here was God's hands touching the lives of men.

OUR SUBSTITUTE

Jesus lived a totally sinless life, devoid of any curse or death seed within Him. This same Man was wrongly condemned to a brutal death, and nailed to the Cross on Calvary's hill. But it was all a part of the divine plan—that one righteous Man should die for the sins of the people so that the entire race of man should not perish before God (John 11:49-52).

While on that rugged Cross, Jesus became sin for us in our place—going to Calvary as our Substitute. He Who knew no sin willingly took all of our sins upon Himself. He, indeed, was a Vessel of Honor fit for the Master's use. Oh the wisdom and greatness of our God!

Christ died an agonizing death separated from His Father

and went into the pit of hell as a mortal man without God—having become the curse of the law, though none of it His own.

"PAID IN FULL!"

Jesus preached to the Old Testament saints a triumphant message. He satisfied the courts of heaven where sin was concerned and God Almighty declared, "Enough! Paid in Full!"

Yes, Satan had taken Jesus into his domain of darkness—into the blazes of hell itself, but Jesus was not guilty of any transgression. Death is only the *wages* of sin! And that was our sin He was carrying!

It was our failure that took Jesus to the Cross. Yet all these things were in the eternal plan that was hidden from the beginning of time.

The Holy Spirit entered hell itself like a Mighty Rushing Wind—much as He did in the book of Acts—and resurrected His Spirit. He became the First Born from the Dead!

The Holy Spirit entered into hell itself like a Mighty Rushing Wind.

This was not the first time a man had been raised from the dead, but He was the prototype of resurrecting spiritually dead men and recreating them back into the image of Almighty God! Glory to the Father! Isn't He outstanding?

*For whom He foreknew, He also predestined
to be conformed to the image of His Son, that He
might be the firstborn among many brethren.*
ROMANS 8:29

23

Jesus took the keys of death and hell from their leader, then came up out of the pit of hell and passed through the earth. He grabbed His body from the grave and ascended before the very throne of God. This Lord Jesus presented His spotless Blood before God Almighty as a propitiation—as a ransom to deliver mankind. The payment was more than enough! His Blood carried the very life of God that was poured out for us!

> *And if you call on the Father, who without*
> *partiality judges according to each one's work,*
> *conduct yourselves throughout the time of your stay*
> *here in fear; knowing that you were not redeemed with*
> *corruptible things, like silver or gold, from your aimless*
> *conduct received by tradition from your fathers, but*
> *with the precious blood of Christ, as of a lamb*
> *without blemish and without spot.*
> I PETER 1:17-19

God accepted His Blood; it satisfied in full the debt of sin against mankind. His Blood was then poured out on the Mercy Seat in Heaven's Holy of Holies—God did all of this for us!

It wasn't for Himself, but for you and me! Think of it! It was for men who could never have paid enough to walk free of sin—who could never have prayed long enough—who could never have done anything to break the power of the devil over our lives!

HE FORGETS YOUR SIN

Jesus, The Undisputed Champion of our Salvation has paid the eternal price to set us free from sin, death, hell, and the grave. Glory! Glory!

Mankind has been JUSTIFIED! *Just-as-if* we had never, ever committed sin. We've been set free by the precious Blood of the Lamb of God! Our debt has been paid in full and the Great Judge of the Universe has declared us justified!

Those of us who have been born again have received our justification before Almighty God and eternal life has been imparted into our spirits.

In the Bible, our Gracious Father has declared that the only thing He forgets are the sins of the ones who trust in His great salvation. God is omniscient: that is, He knows all things in times past, present, and future. But He willfully chooses to forget the sins of man once the Redeeming Blood is applied.

NAILED TO THE CROSS!

God does not see born again believers as forgiven sinners, rather as those who have *never* sinned.

Religion has taught us that we are "sinners saved by grace." Yes, at one time we were spiritually dead because of iniquity—and it's true we were saved by God's grace and mercy, but in His eyes now, we are no longer sinners. In God's sight we have no past! We are now clean, justified sons and daughters of the Almighty!

> *And you, being dead in your trespasses and the*
> *uncircumcision of your flesh, He has made alive*
> *together with Him, having forgiven you all trespasses,*
> *having wiped out the handwriting of requirements that was*
> *against us, which was contrary to us. And He has taken*
> *it out of the way, having nailed it to the cross.*
>
> COLOSSIANS 2:13-14

Our Precious Jesus reconciled us to our Father. Though

25

we were spirituually dead and eternally separated from God because of sin, God forgave us because of the work of Jesus done on the Cross of Calvary and in His resurrection.

The Father, because of our Lord Jesus, was able to blot out every evidence of sin—eradicate it by the Blood of the Lamb of God by nailing the entire *sin nature* to the Cross. Praise God!

COMPLETELY COMMITTED

What a plan! Let me repeat it once more: in His eyes, the moment we are born again we have no past. We do not enter the Kingdom of God as a forgiven sinner, but rather as one justified before the Lord as if we'd never sinned at all—sons and daughters of God! We truly are brand new creatures; old things have passed away from us!

> *We do not enter the Kingdom of God as a forgiven sinner, but rather as one justified before the Lord as if we'd never sinned at all.*

From His heart, God chose to send the Redeemer to break the power of darkness over His creation. He's the One Who sent Jesus to satisfy the courts of heaven for the transgressions of mankind. It was God's heart Who chose to make us "just" before Him. No one twisted His arm or applied pressure on Him to act. It was His decision to deliver us from the coming wrath. He *loves* us! We may be flippant when we use that word, but God's love is true and real and everlasting!

Remarkably, He is *completely committed* to us! He desires that every man and woman be delivered and set free—so He personally makes the way of escape an easy way. In fact, it's so simple we often miss it.

CONFESS IT!

The finished work of Calvary has already been fulfilled and established before The Judge of All. The only thing we need to do is believe in our heart what Jesus did for us through the Cross and His resurrection – and with our mouth declare Him to be our Lord and Savior.

> *...that if you confess with your mouth the Lord Jesus and believe in your heart that God has raised Him from the dead, you will be saved. For with the heart one believes unto righteousness, and with the mouth confession is made unto salvation.*
>
> ROMANS 10:9-10

If you've never done that (made your confession of faith in the Lord Jesus), I want to introduce you to—and give you an opportunity to be reconciled to—this gracious God.

Without Jesus in our heart, every one of us would split hell's gates wide open, and all of us, let's admit it, deserve to have hell as our eternal home.

But here is the Good News of the Gospel! Because we could do nothing of ourselves about our sin, He came *to* us, *for* us, and *like* us. Jesus Himself did not need what was accomplished on the Cross—He was sinless. Yet He came just for you and me.

IT'S YOUR DECISION

I hope you realize you can be released from the chains that have held you in bondage for years. The heavy weight of sin and guilt can be lifted from you—and you can truly go free! Will you make that decision and pray with me right now?

27

"Father, I come to you in the Name of Jesus. I know I am a sinner—forgive me. I believe Jesus Christ is Your Son, and that He bore my sin on the Cross of Calvary. I believe He went to hell for me as my Substitute. I believe He has been raised from the dead, alive forevermore. Jesus, come into my heart – live big within me—change me—mold me—make me new and right before You. I declare You to be my Lord and Savior. I yield myself to You, Lord Jesus. I renounce my past. Thank you Father, that according to Your Word, You have saved me! I am born again into the family of God. In Jesus name, Amen!"

You have just made the most important decision you will ever make! You have begun the greatest journey imaginable! As a member of His household, you are now an heir of the inheritance that He has had held for you since the beginning of time. Life is so wonderful in Him.

Again I say welcome. Now, follow me as we continue to talk about justification.

HE CANNOT LIE

When we come to our God Who says, "I cannot lie"—not that He *won't* lie, but that He *cannot* lie—and He says we are justified before Him, that takes a major step of faith to accept and walk in it.

We often think we have to "do something" to be justified – to demonstrate what our brain says is *good enough* behavior for this to happen. And we punish ourselves by trying to match up with what we think God wants. When, in truth, all He desires is for us to believe Him—to know in our hearts that He didn't lie to us. All the Father wants is that we believe He did what He said He would do for us!—that what he declares He will do, because He is faithful and is not a man that He should lie!

The Lord says our past is gone! He won't ever bring it up to us again. Our yesterday is nothing more than a memory that now needs to be purged and erased from our minds. Praise God forever!

IT IS SETTLED

What the Father has done for us in Jesus Christ of Nazareth is marvelous! So wonderful, in fact, that it is hard for us to seize it and live it out. Yet that's what faith is—taking what God has declared in His written Word, accepting that Word as spoken out of Jehovah's own mouth, and believing it regardless of what we think, feel, or see.

The Lord says we are forgiven; so we accept and believe that! His Word settles the issue. He says when we are saved, we have heaven as our home. He declares we are no longer strangers and foreigners but now belong in the household of God.

We are no longer strangers and foreigners but now belong to the household of God!

Truly, the Blood of Jesus has brought us near to God (Ephesians 2:17). That is so wonderful.

I tell you, this is shouting ground! If we can yell and scream over our favorite football team or because a little white ball on the golf course goes into the hole, surely there is something, somewhere inside of us that must shout—because hell no longer has a hold over us!

For the most part, the Church does not cry out "Hallelujah!" because we do not know who we are or what

Jesus has done for us.

A NEW WALK!

Think how gracious the Lord is. We have been alienated from the life of the Father through our ignorance of His mighty Word! But thank God, we are not going to remain that way. We are going to walk in the Light of His Truth and change from glory to glory. We are free from the authority of darkness and have been translated into the Kingdom of His dear Son—and we are going to walk that way! Praise God!

The resurrection of Jesus is the guarantee of our justification. Had He not risen from the grave, the payment for justification would not have taken place. But He did – He is alive. His Blood has been shed. And the Life of God in the Blood that has been poured out on the mercy seat cries "Mercy!" before the One Who gave Himself for us.

ONLY THE BEGINNING!

We are...recreated back into the image of God with eternal life in our bosom before we die physically!

Because Jesus lives, abundant life is ours. Christ died that we could be separated from our past and walk in eternal life while on this planet. Amazingly, He chose to give us this higher life on *this side* of our physical death. In other words, we are loosed from sin, we are resurrected, and recreated back into the image of God with eternal life in our bosom before we die physically!

Justification paid the debt we owed because of sin and released us from our past.

Because Jesus was our Substitute, God saw us crucified

30

on the Cross with Him, something we will discuss later in this book.

So, in the light of all He has done for us, don't just "make it"—just barely living for God. Go overboard and live abundantly! Sell out to Him! He surely did not withhold anything from us.

As wonderful as justification is for you and me, it's only the beginning! Out of justification comes righteousness—God's greatest gift to us through our Lord Jesus Christ.

CHAPTER 3

*W*HAT IS RIGHTEOUSNESS?

*H*ow can a holy righteous God accept sinful man? How can God justify us? How can He make it permissible for us to stand in His presence after what we have done? That's what Job wanted to know.

> *How then can man be righteous before God?*
> *Or how can he be pure who is born of a woman?*
> JOB 25:4

As the death seed entered mankind, as it passed from generation to generation, and sin filled the atmosphere, it seemed an impossibility to accomplish such a thing. But, in truth, reconciliation and restoration were foremost in the plan of God! In the last chapter, we talked about the process of justifying the ungodly and what God did out of His own heart's desire. Justification is a work of *His* hand.

The Great Judge of All has proclaimed, declared, and decreed that man is justified before Him because of the Blood of the Lamb that was poured out from the Body of our Lord

Jesus. This grace paved a way for you and me to once again come back into the presence of God and have intimate fellowship with Him. You see, the Father so desperately wanted us back, He, Himself, paid the debt that was on each one of our heads. How can we understand and grasp such a marvelous work? That a Holy God would love the human race so much that He would die for us—the Sinless for the sinner. Truly, His mercy is unfathomable!

Yet, justification was only the beginning of this grace that has flowed toward us through the ages. Just as Scripture relates that God had to release the Children of Israel out of the bondage of Egypt to bring them into the promised land, that's what He has also done for us.

IT'S NOT A BEHAVIOR

Justification released us from the bondage of sin and death that held us captive so that He could bring us into a right position with Him where His divine blessings abound. Out of justification comes righteousness.

For He made him who knew no sin to be sin for us,
that we might become the righteousness of God in Him.

2 CORINTHIANS 5:21

Righteousness in simplicity is right-standing with God. It is something we *become*; who we are in the eyes of God. It is not a behavior, rather the ability to come and stand in the presence of God Almighty—to approach the very throne of God without guilt, condemnation, or inferiority.

Righteousness in simplicity is right-standing with God.

Most of the Church world knows nothing about this marvelous blessing. Many Christians think of themselves as unworthy no-goods who go before the Father begging, pleading—hoping maybe somewhere, someday they might talk Him into doing something for them *if* they implore and cry long enough.

This kind of behavior is completely contrary to the Word of God! We have such a loving Father, so filled with grace, that He not only invites us, but commands us to come boldly before Him to receive what we need because we have a High Priest well familiar with our human weaknesses.

For we do not have a High Priest who cannot sympathize with our weaknesses, but was in all points tempted as we are, yet without sin. Let us therefore come boldly to the throne of grace, that we may obtain mercy and find grace to help in time of need.

HEBREWS 4:15,16

Read it again! We've been instructed to come boldly, *not arrogantly*, but boldly to the Throne of Grace—to the Mercy Seat itself, where the Blood of Jesus was poured out for you and me to not just hope, but *obtain* the mercy and grace we need.

That Mercy Seat in the heavenly Holy of Holies was made for us. It certainly wasn't made for Him. He didn't need it except that it was necessary to reconcile us back into His presence. Righteousness places us in a position to come before Him as kings and priests without the guilt and shame that has plagued us for years.

WE'RE AT GOD'S TABLE

Most people struggle with inferiority, which is one reason

34

why we miss the blessings of God. Without knowing and accepting our rightful place—welcomed at His side and in His presence because of the righteousness He gave us—we stay at a distance because we are afraid. We are much like Adam and Eve after the fall!

Scripture says that God has prepared a table before us in the presence of our enemies (Psalm 23). Obviously, that is not a heavenly feast, but one here on this earth because we have no enemies in heaven. However, instead of sitting at the table He has prepared, we are crawling around on our hands and knees, hoping we might be able to grab some morsel of blessing that hits the floor!

Righteousness sits us at the table with God Almighty, not as beggars but as kings and priests!

Righteousness sits us at the table with God Almighty, not as beggars but as kings and priests! Do you see how we have missed it?

Guilt and condemnation bring inferiority. I'm sorry to say that we have been taught these things in Church by the hell, fire, and damnation messages we've all heard. Yes, we agree that we *should* go to hell, but thank God for His grace and mercy. Praise Him for the Good News of the Gospel. That is exactly why Jesus came; to set us free and lift us back into His presence, up at His level!

IN HEAVENLY PLACES

Oh, the goodness of God is beyond anything we could ever hope or dream! I love knowing that He didn't want anyone to go to hell and that He made a way for us to escape the penalty we so rightly deserved. I am thrilled to know that He is not mad, or just waiting to thrust His wrath at us when we make mistakes!

Our Father loves us and knows the frailty of our flesh. He knows how broken and messed up we are and yet, still offers His love. That is why He made a provision for us to come out of that sin nature—to be loosed from Satan's grip—to wipe away our past so that we may be seated with Him in heavenly places! Glory to God!

Our Father loves us and knows the frailty of our flesh.

It is awful to live our entire life in condemnation—afraid to approach our Father. It's dreadful to live eaten up with guilt when God has declared us righteous before Him! No, we didn't commit any righteousness among our sin and Jesus didn't commit any sin in the midst of His righteousness. We were totally sinful and He was totally righteous. But let's look at 2 Corinthians 5:21 again.

For He [God] made Him [Jesus] who knew no sin to be sin for us, that we might become the righteousness of God in Him. [inserts mine]
2 CORINTHIANS 5:21

Jesus didn't commit any sin but was made to be *our* sin. He took our iniquity so that He could give us His right-standing with the Father. Think about that! It's not that we *are* righteous, but that God *declares* us to be righteous in His sight because of the sacrifice of Jesus on the Cross of Calvary we accept in our hearts. What a God we serve!

TOO GOOD TO BE TRUE?

The devil strives hard to keep us heavily weighted with the guilt and condemnation of our past, when in truth, God has wiped it away. There is no evidence of our past.

Righteousness is so marvelous it can hardly be fathomed. It can only be comprehended by faith deep in our spirit.

Our carnal mind can't even begin to understand the wonders of being in right-standing with God. It sounds too good to be true because we know how we've been—we know what we've done and how we have acted—and what our life has been like with all it's failures. We know ourselves!

Yet, God has declared us righteous and He is not a man that He should lie. With our own mouth we need to start declaring that we are the righteousness of God in Christ Jesus. *He* is the One Who declared it; we are just agreeing with Him!

The first few times we are bold enough to even attempt to say such a thing, our knees may be knocking so loud others may hear them. But God is the One Who said we are in right standing with Him. *He* accomplished the work. We just need to agree with Him, believe what He said, and enter in.

BREAKING SATAN'S POWER

Once we are born again, Romans 6 says that the hold of sin is broken in our lives. Justification declares that sin shall no longer lord it over us.

Satan does not have the power to make us continue sinning because his authority has been completely broken where we are concerned. He only has the ability to suggest sinful behavior in our weak areas. He merely comes and says things to us that we are already leaning toward anyway. He keeps whispering in our ears and counts on us to yield to his suggestions. But he surely cannot *make* us sin.

Yet he has something almost as devious and just as effective as iniquity itself. If we won't sin, then he keeps us thinking *about* sin—our past failures, what others have done to us, or keeps us watching everybody else's iniquity. That is called being sin-conscious.

People who murmur and gossip fall into this category. Sin-consciousness causes them to feel inferior, so they try to make themselves look better by pointing out the flaws of others.

Such people have a real problem with their own self worth—and it's why they talk about everyone else. It keeps the attention off of themselves and their own imperfections. People who stay tuned to themselves and how "nobody understands" them and their problems have an inferiority complex.

These saints do not understand righteousness, nor what God has done for His people through it. They are guilt and condemnation conscious. They are aware of what believers *ought* to be, but like to point out how you've missed the mark while keeping silent about their own mistakes.

GRACE! GRACE!

The more we center on our weaknesses, the more our weaknesses show up in our life—and that is why we never seem to break free of them. We must stay focused on righteousness and the work of God's hand in our lives. Our whole intent is to grow in the things of God—to become more conformed to the image of our Father's Dear Son.

Deliberate, habitual sin is not becoming nor natural to believers. Too many misuse God's grace—sloppily and cheaply—when it is neither. Grace toward man cost God His Son on the Cross of Calvary! And when we begin to be truly thankful for His grace in our lives and appreciate it, then we'll handle both sin and grace differently.

If we can ever understand righteousness (to forget about our sin and let His Blood be sufficient), then, my friend, we can go on. We need to quit examining everyone else and deal with our own defects in the light of righteousness and the power of the Blood.

Once this is understood, murmuring and backbiting would cease in the churches. It's the *inferiorities* within us, the things we won't turn loose of, that make us point out the problems of others. The Almighty has declared us in right standing with Him so we can come before Him without guilt, condemnation, or inferiority!

NO MORE GUILT

Righteousness pushes back darkness and brings us to greater heights in Him. When we can clearly "see" that all guilt is gone and that we truly can stand before God Who is holy and pure and spotless; if we can look beyond the frailties we know we all have and be what He has declared; we are on the path to victory!

God has declared us in right standing with Him so that we can come before our awesome God without guilt, condemnation, or inferiority!

The only way we escape from the condemnation, guilt, and inferiority that has driven us all of our lives is by faith that God meant what He said and by staking our life on that Word. Righteousness makes us a king and priest before God, Himself!

IS IT POSSIBLE?

I know what some of you are saying, "There is none righteous, no, not one." and, "All have sinned and fall short of the glory of God."

Let's examine the first part. Yes, that verse can be found in Romans 3:10, but He is talking about the unregenerate

39

man, people who do not seek after God. In the next verses, He says their throats are open sepulchers and that their feet are swift to shed blood, and that there is no fear of God before their eyes. Is that a picture of God's true people? No, they are not symptomatic of authentic Christian behavior throughout the New Testament. Such conduct contradicts the Words of our Father for Godly living.

Now let's take a look at that second statement: that all have sinned and fall short of the glory of God. It can be found in verse 23 of that same chapter, but let's read it in context. This passage of Scripture wasn't even talking about sin.

> *But now the righteousness of God apart from the law is revealed, being witnessed by the Law and the Prophets, even the righteousness of God, through faith in Jesus Christ, to all and on all who believe. For there is no difference; for all have sinned and fall short of the glory of God, being justified freely by His grace through the redemption that is in Christ Jesus, whom God set forth as a propitiation by His blood, through faith, to demonstrate His righteousness, because in His forbearance God had passed over the sins that were previously committed, to demonstrate at the present time His righteousness, that He might be just and the justifier of the one who has faith in Jesus.*
> ROMANS 3:21-26

These verses tell us that His righteousness comes *to* all and *on* all who have faith in Jesus Christ. And that righteousness comes to those who believe *because* we have all sinned and fallen short of God's glory!

IT'S SETTLED!

The Word declares that God justifies freely by grace those

who have faith in the Blood that was shed on Calvary's Cross —so that He may pass over and ignore former sins without punishment! The Amplified Bible says that God Himself is righteous and that He justifies and accepts as righteous him who has [true] faith in Jesus (vs. 26). Glory to God! Righteousness has come upon all who have been born again into this Great Family—it had to, for God is no respecter of persons and all of us have missed the mark. My brothers and sisters, it's settled!

God is not upset with us, but He has made it possible for everyone to come into His presence without guilt, condemnation, or inferiority. Praise God forevermore!

For if by the one man's offense death reigned through the one, much more those who receive abundance of grace and of the gift of righteousness will reign in life through the One, Jesus Christ.

ROMANS 5:17

Here is the same verse in the Amplified Bible:

For if because of one man's trespass (lapse, offense) death reigned through that one, much more surely will those who receive [God's] overflowing grace (unmerited favor) and the free gift of righteousness [putting them into right standing with Himself] reign as kings in life through the one Man Jesus Christ (the Messiah, the Anointed One).

Death had passed to all mankind because of Adam's transgression in the Garden. And it reigned supreme over each man's life. It was one hundred percent effective with no option of escape for anybody. But *much more surely* than the

41

grip death had on us, those who will receive God's overflowing grace and walk in His free gift of righteousness can reign in this world as kings over the circumstances of life by the Man, Jesus Christ—in truth, the Word of the Living God!

By operating from this gracious position with our Father, we can speak the Words of God and rule as kings over the kingdom of darkness! Can we grasp such a marvelous thing?

GOD DECLARED IT!

We are righteous in the eyes of God Almighty. It is something He, Himself, has accomplished in the lives of each one of His people.

Righteousness is a natural by-product of the justification process. So when we say, "We are righteous" that is not a faith statement, but truth based on the Word of God and the fact that He cannot lie!

If we are born again, from God's point of view, we are righteous.

If we are born again, from God's point of view, we are righteous. And remember this: we cannot get to be *more* righteous or *less* righteous—we are simply in right-standing with God.

If we say, "I am a Christian" then in the same breath, we should say, "I am righteous" because they are one in the same. We can't be a Christian without being righteous and if we are righteous, we are Christians.

Religion has made righteousness one of those Sunday School words that might be attainable in the distant future—something we have to work toward, when we, in fact, are declared righteous by the new birth!

DON'T BE FOOLED!

By saying Christians can be defeated, Satan has sold us a big lie. We should *never* be defeated! Christian means "little Christ" or "Christ-like" and He most assuredly is not conquered and crushed.

So why is it that we have so many defeated, born again, Holy Ghost filled believers? I am convinced it is because we don't know who we are! We simply don't comprehend what the Father has done for us.

Scripture declares that God's people are destroyed for a lack of knowledge—and because we are in ignorance, we've bought a lie. We have believed there was no way we could ever be righteous—that we don't have the ability—that the Word really doesn't mean what it says. Therefore, we have never *walked out* who we are in Christ Jesus—justified and in right-standing with the Father.

Remember, it was God's full intention from the beginning to break the power of darkness over His creation and bring them back into the glory of their original condition. And that includes, while always subordinate and obedient to Almighty God, ruling and reigning as kings on this planet.

We are not to be out there somewhere just doing our own thing or pressing our own agenda. No! We are to rightly discern the will of God—take His Words—speak them as a king and rule over circumstances so that His will can be done on earth as it is in heaven. But we will never step out and do that without a revelation so real and deep within us that it wipes away every doubt that we, indeed, are righteous before God through Christ Jesus!

OUR IMAGE OF GOD

Hebrews says that we are to come *boldly* to the Throne of Grace. We are invited to walk right in the door where God lives, go through the curtain of the flesh of His Son Jesus—knowing that we are totally accepted there without condemnation, inferiority, or guilt. But, if that truth is not real to us, if we don't know who we are, we won't live like the kings that God has created us to be. We'll spend our time trying to maybe, one day, get the ear of God—just hoping He will answer our prayers.

People by the thousands try to attract the Father's attention, then become depressed because nothing is working in their lives, and leave the Church. Most of the time, they leave because people sitting in the pews, who think they "know" but are ignorant of God and His ways, put some guilt trip on the new Christian who is trying to grow in the things of God.

Such people make the Christian life seem too difficult and too hard. They make God to be judgmental, ready to strike some kind of destruction on us every time we slip. The "babe in Christ" leaves, thinking they could never walk this life the Creator expects.

All of this deceit has come out of the carnal, religious attitudes of self-righteous Christians who have no understanding of God's compassion nor what He has accomplished for us. These are lies straight out of hell!

WHICH GROUP?

You see, there are different groups within the Church.

First, there are those who are serious in their walk with the Lord and strive in every area to be what He wants them to be by the Word of God.

Next, there is a group that is "playing" church, but when the services are over, they have no intention of growing in Christ. They merely act "right" at the House of God, but intend to go home and do just as they please. They only want to have an image and they use the Church to achieve that objective.

Finally, there are people who desire to go on with God and dig deep into His Word and be what He wants them to be. Yet, the religious lies they have accepted have made it a "works" mentality until, in their minds, the proper Christian lifestyle becomes too difficult to live out.

BELIEVE IT!

I am convinced that at least ninety percent of the Church is not living as God intends. They are striving—hoping one day to be accepted and have favor with the Father—all because they don't know who they are. If we can understand the fact that we don't have to work to be righteous—to make our sins disappear, or to get out of condemnation—then we can begin to live like the righteous sons and daughters of the Great Jehovah God we have been declared to be.

The concept that we have the same right-standing with God as Jesus is mind-boggling!

We must receive this gift of righteousness by faith to be able to reign in life as stated in Romans 5:17. It takes faith to accept what Jesus did for us and walk in it because the idea itself is so marvelous. The concept that we have the same right-standing with God as Jesus is mind-boggling! But at some point, for us to walk in the benefits of righteousness, we've got to believe! Again, we must accept the Words of God as truth because He cannot lie! And His Word is the law of this land!

The devil is a liar. He has deceived the Church and has taught that righteousness is based on whether or not we wear make-up or how long we keep our hair. We've dreamed about being righteous, but thought it to be something beyond our reach when in reality it's what we are in the eyes of God.

The Church has even helped the devil and kept the majority of the people ignorant of this fabulous truth. Many in the pulpit are guilty of teaching things about God not found in the Word.

"NO MORE!"

We need to know that the Almighty is a holy, righteous, kind, loving Father. He is for us—not against us. He so desires that His people live in the victory and the blessings He has provided, that He gave His own Son to destroy the works of the devil. He has made it possible for us to look hell square in the face and say, "No! No more!"

The Lord has set us free, cleaned us up, redeemed and justified us in the courts of heaven and given us an open invitation to come boldly to the Throne of Grace. Why? Because we are now sons and daughters of the Most High God!

Beyond that, righteousness has given us His full armor: His precious Blood, His Mighty Word, His Kingdom authority, His explosive power, and the wonderful Name of Jesus to which every knee must bow! What a God!

Victory is ours because of our Lord Jesus, the Cross of Calvary, and the resurrection! But we must receive God's overflowing grace and this free gift of righteousness—and allow them to work in our lives.

If we walk around in darkness, ignorant of who we are in Christ Jesus and too lazy to find out, Satan will continue to reign in our lives because he moves in darkness.

The Bible says we are complete in Him and righteousness restores us to every single thing God has had for us since before the foundation of the world. Adam lost everything in the garden with his act of treason, but the Last Adam, Jesus, reclaimed it and has placed it in the hands of the Church.

MOVING FORWARD

Once we understand righteousness, we will discover it is a *masterful* thing. It literally puts us as masters over situations in our lives.

Most of us bow and cower like weaklings, failing to stand in the midst of our trials because we don't know who we are.

Each person must make their own decision regarding this truth. For example, I can go on with God in the benefits of righteousness, while you sit back in the pew and just dream of them.

It's my desire that we move forward *together* for this is the will of God; that His people, His Body, rise up and keep the devil under our feet!

Can you imagine the powerhouse the Church would be if we would get serious and take hold of this truth? It is hard to envision what God could accomplish in these last days with a people who knew their rightful position!

Settle this thing forever! As a child of God you are the righteousness of God in Christ Jesus. Walking in righteousness will destroy the sin consciousness that we have wallowed in and it will give us new liberty in prayer. This revelation will bring us back into powerful fellowship with God – allowing us to see ourselves unashamedly as joint heirs with Jesus Christ. It will enable us to work with Him as co-laborers, taking authority over the devil in the Name of Jesus.

Today, He is waiting on us to take from Him what He offers. With total confidence, standing on the Word, we need to wear our robe of righteousness to the glory of God the Father!

CHAPTER 4

THE OLD AND THE NEW!

*W*hat a blessed people we are! God has made us righteous by the Blood of His Son that was shed on Calvary.

For He made Him who knew no sin to be sin for us, that we might become the righteousness of God in Him.

2 CORINTHIANS 5:21

By that gift of righteousness, God Himself enabled us to come boldly into His presence without guilt, condemnation, or inferiority. We truly have an open door into the glory of God Almighty. Once born again, or rather *born from above*, we become a totally new creature in Christ Jesus; one that is created into the exact image of God!

We're not just the same person painted over—not just somebody we have to pretend to be. God in His mercy, completely severed the power of darkness and sin that held each of us in captivity. Through justification God took up residence in these bodies of clay, and put us in right-standing with Him as sons and daughters—so that each member of His family could walk out on earth the life that Jesus exemplified for us. Think of that!

"LIVING STONES"

Through the Blood, the Cross, and the Resurrection of Jesus, He has accomplished everything necessary to perfect and place each of us as "living stones" into the spiritual Temple of His presence here on earth. Each stone is complete in itself with the fullness of the Deity within, yet we are all important integral parts of the bigger corporate Body of Christ—the Church of the Living God!

His people are not only walking mobile temples of His glory, but are also empowered and commissioned to mediate and make this power available for the individual needs of the people as priests. In truth, Jesus has never left. His Spirit has filled each one of His sons and daughters to continue to accomplish the will of the Father.

We are His cherished treasures, the roses in His garden!

What God has desired us to be on this earth is almost beyond our comprehension. But God really does love us! He cares about us and is totally committed to our well being. Our names are written in the palm of His hand. We are His cherished treasures, the roses in His garden! He wants us to show forth to a dying world the power of God.

The Father placed Himself in us so that we could shine so brightly with the glory of His presence that others will be drawn and come to a knowledge of this Wonderful Savior!

BULLS AND GOATS

Righteousness is such an incredible gift. When we can truly grasp what Jesus has done for us and what the goodness of our God has attained for all of mankind, we are going to shout! He is absolutely outstanding.

Righteousness actually existed in the Old Covenant as well as the New. We know that Moses and the prophets had intimate access to God Almighty, yet there is a major difference between the two Covenants.

Righteousness actually existed in the Old Covenant as well as the New.

In the Old Testament, righteousness came through the sacrifices of bulls and goats, but it was only a limited type of righteousness granted to servants. It was not the righteousness that is granted to sons and daughters of the Almighty. Now, we can be servants to God *as* sons or daughters, however, we are not just servants.

LIMITED RIGHTEOUSNESS

You remember, once a year the High Priest entered with fear and trembling into the Holy of Holies with the blood of bulls and goats to sprinkle on the Mercy Seat for the sins of the people. The blood of those sacrificial animals was only a type and symbol of the Blood of The Lamb slain before the foundation of the world, but it was enough to cover the sin and deliver the people for a period of one year. Yet it had to be repeated every year because that blood did not purge the sin, only covered it. Old Testament saints were only servants of the Most High God.

There is a major difference between a servant and a son of God. In the Old Testament, these people were not born again. In fact, no one was born again, even under Jesus' ministry—not until after Calvary, but they had a limited type of righteousness.

The Holy Spirit was not living inside the Old Testament saints; He came only upon those directly commissioned of God – the priests, the kings, and the prophets. As we read the Old Testament stories, there were some amazing and outstanding things that God was able to accomplish through those devout (but unregenerate) men and women. However, if they were able to achieve such things under that inferior covenant, think of what the sons and daughters of the Most High God should be able to do under the New Covenant with the *better* promises!

> *But now He [Jesus] has obtained a more excellent ministry, inasmuch as He is also Mediator of a better covenant, which was established on better promises. For if that first covenant had been faultless, then no place would have been sought for a second. Because finding fault with them, He says: "Behold, the days are coming, says the Lord, when I will make a new covenant with the house of Israel and with the house of Judah—not according to the covenant that I made with their fathers in the day when I took them by the hand to lead them out of the land of Egypt; because they did not continue in My covenant, and I disregarded them, says the Lord."*
>
> HEBREWS 8:6-9

*"For this is the covenant that I will make with
the house of Israel after those days, says the Lord:
I will put My laws in their mind and write them
on their hearts; and I will be their God, and they shall
be My people. None of them shall teach his neighbor,
and none his brother, saying, 'Know the Lord,' for
all shall know Me, from the least of them to the greatest
of them. For I will be merciful to their unrighteousness,
and their sins and their lawless deeds I will remember
no more." In that He says, "A new covenant,"
He has made the first obsolete. Now what
is becoming obsolete and growing old
is ready to vanish away.*

HEBREWS 8:10-13

REMARKABLE SERVANTS!

Let's look at what some of the servants of God achieved —and remember, they were not filled with the Holy Ghost. In fact, they were spiritually dead, unregenerate men!

Noah did a rather good job listening to God about the ark and completing the task exactly as he was instructed. How about Moses? He also did some remarkable things! These two men were servants of God living under limited righteousness! Their sins were not washed away by the Blood of Jesus, nor was the devil at that point defeated!

Have any of you parted a Red Sea lately—or built an ark to save all of life from total destruction? Have you initiated ten plagues to deliver a nation, or gone up on a high mountaintop to sit in the presence of Jehovah while He talks to you and writes His words on two tablets of stone? What about the faithful Joshua? Have any of you parted a river in flood season or marched around a major city and seen the wall collapse at your command? Have you told the sun to stand still and witnessed its obedience to your directive until you had time to win your battle?

These were only servants under a covenant that accepted the blood of bulls and goats!

ONLY A COVERING

How about David? Have any of you seen a Goliath and slung a rock and hit the one and only spot he was vulnerable? What about Gideon? Would you like to take a 300 man army and go against enemy troops that numbered into the multiple thousands—blow a few horns and light a few lamps and see what happens?

Once again, these men had only limited righteousness with Jehovah under the Old Covenant! Would you, like Esther, go before a king knowing full well you could be executed just by reason of walking into his royal pres-

These were only servants under a covenant that accepted the blood of bulls and goats!

ence uninvited? How about Daniel in the lion's den? What about Samson, who with only a bone, slew thousands? Elijah raised people from the dead and stopped the rain for years!

All of the people involved in these Old Testament exploits were servants. None had the Spirit of God living and dwelling within them. None were born again. No one was a child of God, but only justified by the blood of sacrificial animals. Their sin was not wiped out, only covered over.

53

They did not have the power to cast out demons. These things did not become a reality until the completed work of Calvary, because Satan wasn't defeated until then.

WHAT SHOULD WE EXPECT?

If God Almighty bestowed on servants that kind of power —that kind of ability, that kind of reward—what in the world could He accomplish with a son or daughter who is full of the Spirit of the Living God, created back into the image of the Father?

These powerful Old Testament saints were able to perform on this extraordinary level of divine operation because of a limited form of righteousness based on the shed blood of bulls and goats! What should we expect to accomplish with God when the Blood of His very own Son has placed us in full right-standing with God, set us completely free from the kingdom of darkness, and put the devil under our feet? My Lord! Think of what could—and should—happen!

"WHAT WILL PEOPLE THINK?"

The very *least* the Church of the Living God should be doing is what we read about in the Old Testament. In fact, the acts of the New Testament Church should far surpass the excellence of the Old Covenant, as wonderful as it was. Yet it didn't have the power of the Blood of Jesus as its nucleus.

Oh, if the Church would wake up and believe the Word! If we would start trusting our God, take the Word at face value, and be bold enough to step out, there is no telling what God could carry out through this Body in this day and hour!

You may say, "What if I do that and people think I'm crazy?"

Well, what do you think the majority thought of these Old Testament heroes? People said Noah was crazy building an ark—talking about something called rain! It seems it had never rained up to that point. Scripture calls Noah a preacher of righteousness, but nobody listened to him and repented when he preached of the coming destruction. No one believed his message, but there was good news at the end of his story. He rose above the problem at hand, and what others chided him for, ultimately gave him victory!

It's very clear that what the nation of Israel had in the Old Covenant was wonderful. God said, "I'll feed you. I will clothe, protect and sustain you. I will be your God and you will be My people."

We've been grafted into the natural olive tree of Israel.

"BETTER" PROMISES

Those are outstanding promises, but the Bible says that we live under *better* promises than those offered to them.

The verses in Hebrews 8 were not just written to Israel, but also to us because we are spiritual Israel. We've been grafted into the natural olive tree of Israel, so whatever promises belonged to them, now belong to us as well! The Book says that He will be our God and we will be His people and that He will remember our sins no more! That is God talking. He has chosen to forget our failures.

*Now when these things had been thus prepared,
the priests always went into the first part of the
tabernacle, performing the services. But into the
second part the high priest went alone once a year,
not without blood, which he offered for himself and
for the people's sins committed in ignorance; the Holy
Spirit indicating this, that the way into the Holiest of
All was not yet made manifest while the first tabernacle
was still standing. It was symbolic for the present
time in which both gifts and sacrifices are offered
which cannot make him who performed the service
perfect in regard to the conscience—concerned only
with foods and drinks, various washings, and fleshly
ordinances imposed until the time of reformation.*

HEBREWS 9:6-10

*But Christ came as High Priest of the good
things to come, with the greater and more perfect
tabernacle not made with hands, that is, not of this
creation. Not with the blood of goats and calves, but
with His own blood He entered the Most Holy Place
once for all, having obtained eternal redemption. For if the
blood of bulls and goats and the ashes of a heifer, sprinkling
the unclean, sanctifies for the purifying of the flesh, how
much more shall the blood of Christ, who through the eternal
Spirit offered Himself without spot to God, cleanse your
conscience from dead works to serve the living God?*

HEBREWS 9:11-14

The blood of bulls and goats needed to be shed and applied every year. It could not purge their sin, only give them a limited righteousness—yet it absolutely resulted in outstanding feats. They did those exploits under the power of an Old Covenant the Bible states has now been replaced by one that is better! If that sacrificial blood could give them a right-standing with Jehovah that lifted them to the heights of such power—*how much more* shall those of us who come to God, receive our forgiveness by the cleansing power of the Blood of the Lamb, and receive this gift of righteousness, reign in life by the One Man, Jesus Christ? How much more are we equipped to handle the issues of life?

How much more are we equipped to handle the issues of life?

The blood of those animals under the Old Covenant could not make them perfect nor could it cleanse the people of their sin. But the covenant sealed in the Blood of Jesus does. This precious Blood of the Son of God has been poured on the heavenly Mercy Seat for us. And this free gift of righteousness has placed the Church in its God-ordained position. The Father gave us His righteousness—the ability to triumph in the affairs of life! *How much more shall the Blood of Jesus purge your conscience from dead works to serve the Living God?* That is not only righteousness, it is outstanding! Praise God forever!

HIS PRECIOUS BLOOD

Let's keep reading the Word:

Therefore not even the first covenant was dedicated without blood. For when Moses had spoken every precept to all the people according to the law, he took the blood of calves and goats, with water, scarlet wool, and hyssop, and sprinkled both the book itself and all the people, saying, "This is the blood of the covenant which God has commanded you." Then likewise he sprinkled with blood both the tabernacle and all the vessels of the ministry. And according to the law almost all things are purified with blood, and without shedding of blood there is no remission.

HEBREWS 9:18-22

Therefore it was necessary that the copies of the things in the heavens should be purified with these, but the heavenly things themselves with better sacrifices than these. For Christ has not entered the holy places made with hands, which are copies of the true, but into heaven itself, now to appear in the presence of God for us; not that He should offer Himself often, as the high priest enters the Most Holy Place every year with blood of another—He then would have had to suffer often since the foundation of the world; but now, once at the end of the ages, He has appeared to put away sin by the sacrifice of Himself.

HEBREWS 9:23-26

Even in the Old Covenant it took blood to deal with sin. But that was in God's design from the beginning. This is one reason He made man to inhabit a body of flesh, blood and

THE OLD AND THE NEW!

bone. He knew His Blood would have to be poured out from the Messiah as a ransom for mankind.

God revealed His plan line upon line, precept upon precept through the ages, and what He required in the Old Covenant only foreshadowed the true events to which were to follow.

Previously, the high priest would enter the Holiest of All with the blood of the sacrificial animals year after year in the Temple of God made with hands. But when Jesus came into the heavenly Holy of Holies with His precious Blood—having already obtained eternal redemption for us—He appeared once and for all times. And that Blood has not lost its power as it cries from the Mercy Seat to Almighty God on our behalf!

And as it is appointed for men to die once, but after this the judgment, so Christ was offered once to bear the sins of many. To those who eagerly wait for Him He will appear a second time, apart from sin, for salvation.
HEBREWS 9:27-28

To those looking for Him, He will return; not bearing sin again, but as the Champion of our Salvation! The implication is that if we are *not* looking, He will not return for us.

NOT A RELIGION

There is a remnant within the Church—those of us who are hungering and thirsting for this righteousness to fully manifest in our lives. There are believers who are serious about their Christianity. To us, it is not a religion, but a way of life. We want to turn loose of yesterday and its chains, to

> *We want to turn loose of yesterday and its chains, to uphold righteousness and walk uprightly before God and man.*

uphold righteousness and walk uprightly before God and man.

This is the crowd who is looking for Him to come back because they are preparing themselves as a bride would adorn herself for her husband. We prepare by walking uprightly and in holiness.

We need to get our lives together by mortifying the deeds of our flesh and walking in love, whether anyone else does or not.

HOW MUCH MORE!

I am thankful for what God has done in my life. It took a long time to understand what He did, but I don't want to go back to yesterday and its vulgarities. I want to walk in the blessings that eternal life, justification, and righteousness have provided by the New Testament, ratified by the Blood of our Savior. I want to live above situations and circumstances by reigning as a king by the one Man, Christ Jesus—the Word of the Living God!

Scripture states that Moses was 120 years old when he died, but his eyes were not dim nor was his natural strength diminished. Today, we have to fight hard to stay alive to 75! And if God did that for a man who did not have the same covenant, the same divine promises, the same righteousness —*how much more* would He do for someone who has been cleansed by His own Son's Blood if they only knew it? What could He do for a group of people who would make a solid decision to trust Him, believe Him, and go for it all in the Name of the Lord? It's here! It's available! God is waiting on us to seize this abundant life Jesus came to give.

Most assuredly, I say to you, he who believes in Me,
the works that I do he will do also; and greater works
than these he will do, because I go to My Father.
JOHN 14:12

In other words Jesus said, "Man, if you've been taken aback with what I have done at the instruction of My Father, you haven't seen anything yet! You are going to do greater things than these because I will be at the right Hand of the Father on your behalf. I am your Advocate before Him. I may be in heaven, but I will send the Holy Spirit to live and dwell within each of you. And He will come to endue you with power to be the witness of My resurrection! Ah, but your sins will not just be covered, they will be wiped away—obliterated."

WIPED AWAY!

Let's see the completeness of our forgiveness by looking at another Scripture.

And you who were dead in trespasses and in the
uncircumcision of your flesh (your sensuality, your
sinful carnal nature), [God] brought to life together with
[Christ], having [freely] forgiven us all our transgressions,
having cancelled and blotted out and wiped away the
handwriting of the note (bond) with its legal decrees
and demands which was in force and stood against us
(hostile to us). This [note with its regulations, decrees,
and demands] He set aside and cleared completely
out of our way by nailing it to [His] cross.
COLOSSIANS 2:13-14 AMP

Glory to God! Our debt of sin and failure is not just stamped "Paid in full by the Blood of the Lamb," there is now no *record* of our sin! The handwriting of that debt was wiped away having been nailed to the Cross of Calvary. We have been set free, given life, and placed in right-standing with the Great "I Am!" Praise His Name forevermore!

There is now no record of our sin!

We can scarcely perceive what God has in store for His people. However, there is a problem in this Blood-bought Church of Jesus Christ. There are people who do not know they are living in sin. How do we think we are going to control the devil (in our lives or anyone else's) when we have too much of Satan and his hellish traits operating in us!

ONE PURPOSE

The power to be victorious comes from holiness and living uprightly while we walk in the light of the Word of God. You see, it was the Father's full intent that Jesus keep walking on the earth *through* us.

It is not right to say Jesus left. The Original returned home, but we have been made copies—still here to accomplish the will of God on earth as it is being done in heaven.

Jesus had one purpose, one goal. That was to do the will of His Father. He made that central and utmost in His life and let nothing move Him from His objective.

When you and I reach the place that what is most important is our obedience to Almighty God, and to be pleasing in His sight, we will say the same thing: "I am here for one reason only—to do the will of my Father!"

The righteousness of the New Testament sealed in the Blood of Jesus enables, empowers, and equips us to fulfill that goal!

CHAPTER 5

*M*AKING IT WORK

*V*ictory belongs to the Lord! It always has, and always will.

We know because of Jesus' death, burial, and resurrection, He is the King, the Commander and Champion of our Salvation! Jesus is Lord – and He has forever conquered the devil and his schemes.

Anything Christ commands Satan to do, he does—no if's, and's, or but's. That is no surprise. When it comes to our Lord Jesus, we simply *expect* that. In our thinking, it is inconceivable for the devil to attain any kind of victory over the Lord. We *know* Jesus wins every time because He is the Son of God —and He has the keys to death and hell.

However, what we haven't understood is that righteousness opens the door for us to walk in that same victory because *we are* God's sons and daughters!

A TRANSFORMATION

Righteousness is not only God's greatest gift to us through Jesus Christ, but it is one of His most outstanding achievements! He took sin-filled, broken people like you and me, whose hearts were bent toward evil, and performed a transforming work. As He came to dwell within our hearts, the power of darkness that imprisoned us was broken!

Out of His own good pleasure, God, through Jesus Christ, delivered us from the domain of sickness, sin, fear, lack, death and translated us into the Kingdom of His Dear Son! We've been adopted into this Royal Family whose victory is assured.

Almighty God has placed a robe of righteousness and the ring of kingdom authority on each one of us. We've been given the awesome privilege to use that exalted Name of Jesus to Whom every knee must bow! And what's more, I believe our Father has declared over us—much as He did over Jesus in the River Jordan— "These are My sons and daughters, and devil, you had better listen to them!'"

The Almighty has placed a robe of righteousness and the ring of kingdom authority on each one of us.

Praise God forevermore! This is what righteousness does.

HE "DECLARED" IT

Our right-standing with God is what demands that the devil bow! Oh yes, we have to study the Word and renew our mind to think and act as God does. And we have to pray and keep ourselves free of sin among other responsibilities, but righteousness is what enables us to do any of that.

The Father has declared us righteous. Yet, if we do not understand our position in Christ Jesus within this Kingdom of God nor comprehend and receive this free gift, our lives will be lived as mere men without power.

Freedom and victory are not automatic with the new birth;

65

they come only with a godly and upright lifestyle filled with integrity. Obviously, we must learn what this entails. We have to walk it out if we want it to work for us.

Let me state it as clearly as I know how. We can be born again, Holy Ghost filled, heaven-bound believers, and yet our lives be in such disarray we never see victory of any kind! It may come as a surprise, but there is a cost involved to walk at this higher level – and most of the Christian community has not paid the price.

We are still acting and talking like the old unregenerate man—we have not renewed our minds, nor taken the time to plant the Word of God in our hearts where it has power. In addition, we haven't mortified the deeds of our body or "sold out" to live for Him. We're not walking by faith believing that God really did what He said He would do.

HEAVENLY INSIGHT

Far too often, our lives reflect the fact we don't believe the Word, because when we believe something we put it into practice. To be quite frank, the Church has absolutely not believed God and yet thinks it has!

My people are destroyed for lack of knowledge...
HOSEA 4:6

The literal translation says that God's people are cut off from receiving a blessing because of a lack of knowledge. We are missing what the Father has had for us from the beginning; not walking in the abundant life or the authority He has purchased and given us.

As a result, we are living far beneath our call and the plan He established for us from before the foundation of the world. In short, we are not *walking out* who we really are. Somehow, we have taken the low road instead of the high because we haven't believed what we *did* know and were ignorant of the rest.

Those who do not understand what is rightfully theirs don't pursue it. To be honest, some of us have known what was available to born again children of God, yet we have not claimed it, and it has cost us dearly. But for those who are willing, and actively paying the price, we will become different people as we allow God to transform us.

> *...strengthened with all might, according to His glorious power, for all patience and longsuffering with joy; giving thanks to the Father who has qualified us to be partakers of the inheritance of the saints in the light. He has delivered us from the power of darkness and conveyed us into the kingdom of the Son of His love, in whom we have redemption through His blood, the forgiveness of sins.*
>
> COLOSSIANS 1:11-14

It we truly believe this, we can walk free of Satan's dominion. If we risk to live by faith and press into the things of God, life will be victorious—because Satan has *already* been defeated. Jesus has *already* won the battle and fulfilled everything necessary to set us free. The only thing He has not done is to make our decisions—that is left entirely up to you and me.

KNOW IT! LIVE IT!

Millions know *about* the things of God, but they haven't become real to them. The kind of life we are talking about apparently seems too good to be true to the average Christian and most perceive this lifestyle as too hard or unattainable.

It's obvious, since many in the Church are still wallowing in the world of flesh.

Far too many Christians are involved in the works of hell —in the realm of darkness—yet, we are supposed to be living in the Kingdom of Light. We are involved in activities we know are inappropriate; trying to get away with as much as we can, all because God and His Kingdom are not real to us.

SHEER DESPERATION

To be honest, what brought me to the reality of God was desperation. I lived a hellish life, perhaps just as you did. Out of sheer despair, I cast myself upon Him because I knew no one could help me *but* Him. The Lord then became a living reality and the Word of God began to speak to me.

> *Out of sheer despair, I cast myself upon Him because I knew no one could help me but Him.*

Within time, the truth of His Word in my heart began to take precedence over the situations in my life until I was certain that God really did love me. This truth persuaded me that God really was bigger than any situation I faced.

I began to gently reach out in trust —area by area—and believe Him to turn my life around. Slowly, but surely, He began to transform me.

My responsibility was to study God's Word and renew my mind. It was my task to pay the price with my time and attention tuned toward the heavenly realm, to change where I went, and to correct the words coming out of my mouth. Occasionally, I even had to change my old friends for those who would encourage me to walk this new life with God.

I continued to fill my mouth and heart with the Word of

the Living God and when adverse circumstances would surface, words such as these would bubble up from my spirit and roll off my tongue: "No you won't Satan – the Greater One is in me!" "My God is working on my behalf and will turn this thing around."

By speaking the Word *over* situations, we bring Him *into* the situations. Please understand that He is already in our lives, but He doesn't manifest Himself unless we invite Him – and recognize that He is there by speaking His truths.

By physically declaring the Word of God, we establish His Kingdom reign over the circumstances we are facing and allow Him to take charge. When we begin to do that on a regular basis, we view *everything* differently.

ASK YOURSELF!

Friend, God does not force us to let Him take control, nor does He constrain us to think and speak His Word. That is left completely in our hands!

The question is: "How do we perceive God"? Is our Creator weak, wishy-washy, or short on power to deliver? Do we see Him as hard-hearted and lacking compassion, refusing to heal, liberate, or set us free? Do we meditate on Him and the Holy Scriptures until deep within us He towers high above life's situations, or do we see our problems as insurmountable even with God?

Are we trusting His Words to be the solution to our dilemmas knowing that God cannot and will not lie? Are we accepting His Word as final authority no matter what the circumstances? I admonish you to search deep within yourself and be honest. Do you really trust God? Have you brought Him into your world? Or do you find yourself in despair as you face the issues of life?

HE PROMISES, HE PERFORMS

Righteousness elevates us to a place with God so that all of heaven's resources are at our disposal. Yet, our doubts are a major reason many find themselves up against a brick wall, unable to move forward.

We fail to make God's presence an actuality, and just squall and bawl over our problems, forgetting that our Father is faithful to perform His Word. It slips our mind that He is the One Who walks through brick walls to fulfill His divine purpose!

Basically, we have lived our lives as if we were in this world without a Savior—and that is not true. We have to know within us that Almighty God is bigger than any situation; *I mean really know it!*

He is not only *able*, but *willing* to do whatever is necessary to bring victory when we are truly believing His Word—contrary to anything we may see with our natural eyes.

I remind you that Scripture states the things we can see in the natural are temporal. In other words, they are subject to change (2 Corinthians 4:17,18).

God's love for us, His power in us, and His presence must be beyond question. These issues must be settled.

RULING AS A KING

To live righteously is to conform to the will of the Father in thought, purpose, and action. God's Word *is* God's will. He doesn't say one thing and mean another.

We have been bought with a price, purchased by the precious Blood of Jesus. The kingdom of darkness no longer has any claim on us—*unless* we give it authority to rule and reign. But if we will receive this abundance of grace and His free gift of righteousness, we can rule as kings in life by Jesus

Christ, the Word of the Living God.

Believing, speaking, and acting on the Word is what brings victory because it is the power of God unto our salvation (Romans 1:16).

> *Then Jesus said to those Jews who believed*
> *Him, "If you abide in My word, you are My*
> *disciples indeed. And you shall know the truth*
> *and the truth shall make you free."*
>
> JOHN 8:31-32

Abiding, and living in the reality of the Word reveals truth to us. The truth we *do* and *abide in* is what sets us free!

It's not enough just to *know* the truth. We must receive it, walk in it and allow it to become a reality.

BREAKING CHAINS

Satan cannot take us captive without our cooperation because his power has been broken over us. He doesn't have the legal right to enter our house and tear things up any time he wants to—unless we open the door and work with him through ignorance, deception, or laziness. We have been completely removed out of his realm of authority.

> *Satan cannot take us captive without our cooperation because his power has been broken over us.*

Justification delivers us, not only from Satan's kingdom, but also from his *power*. We're free from the chains that have held us hostage!

Righteousness, on the other hand, connects us to God to walk upright, holy, sanctified lives. Still, we have to make choices that steer our lives toward that desired end because we can *be* righteous, yet not *live* righteous.

It is imperative that we know who we are in Christ Jesus. Let me say it this way. All of us live each day based on who we think we are—what we have told ourselves, what we have accepted from others, and what we have decided to be truth and reality. Scripture states that as a man thinks in his heart, so is he. So walking in victory is greatly determined by whether we believe we are victorious or not.

Our ability to walk free of condemnation is based on whether we believe we've been set free from it. You see, we all have a "believer" built within us by God so we are believing something all the time, but it is crucial that we believe the *right* thing if we want our lives to grow and flourish. We can be sincere in our beliefs, yet be sincerely wrong – and it will be reflected in our lives.

IT'S IMPLANTED!

Righteous is who we are and it comes with a lifestyle. It is a belief system based on a trust in the Lord that He Who knew no sin became sin for us that we might become the righteousness of God in Him (2 Corinthians 5:21).

Remember, righteousness is the nature of God imparted to us.

> *...for the kingdom of God is not eating and drinking,*
> *but righteousness and peace and joy in the Holy Spirit.*
> ROMANS 14:17

Righteousness manifests itself as joy and peace in the Holy Ghost, because when we finally rise up out of the miry pit and recognize who we are, great joy enters our lives. We realize, "My God! I've been living like the devil. I have missed all the things God has freely given to make me whole. I've been liberated all the time, yet I have let the devil dominate me!" And out of that unspeakable joy flows peace – peace with God and with ourselves.

WALKING THE WALK

Two areas we need to carefully monitor are our mouths and our attitudes. We can wound with words, but even without one spoken word, our attitude can offend. There are things we have to change and choices we need to redirect. But when we begin to *move* in righteousness—and remember, its power is released as we act on and abide in its truths—we become free to *walk* in righteousness allowing the glory of God to begin manifesting.

If we are not abiding in fellowship with God, we lose a sense of His righteousness.

If we are not abiding in fellowship with God, we lose a sense of His righteousness—that close connection that opens the gate for His power to flow. But when we are endeavoring to please Him, we won't be trying to "get away" with anything and subsequently grieve the Spirit of Grace with our sinful conduct. We won't be doing things "under the table"—or cooling things in our refrigerator that shouldn't be there—or hiding things under our bed that are offensive to our Father.

Obviously, we can't go around calling ourselves righteous when we are living in sin. I am talking about holiness; that is, living uprightly before God and man. *Righteous* is who we are in the eyes of God, and righteousness enables us to live holy in the face of God.

73

"FORGIVE ME"

Although the desire to sin may dwell in our physical body, it is not sin until we have consented to an act that is forbidden in the Word of God.

All kinds of thoughts can pass through our head—even hideous ones. What enters our mind will not send us to hell, yet we cannot continue to entertain such thoughts. We have to be aggressive and start squaring our shoulders, declaring "I am righteous"—and alter the way we think. Thoughts that are not put into action die unborn.

We must begin to change the way we relate to people— what we do and how we talk. Also, we must choose to stop taking advantage of people. And when we act like a fool, we need to quickly make it right with God and man, saying "forgive me."

It's a matter of centering in on righteousness and how God wants us to act. He longs to fill this earth with His glory, to the degree that this dying world absolutely falls on their knees in reverence before Him! He wants mankind to see His manifested presence—and we, the Body of Christ, are the ones chosen by God to reveal His goodness to them.

A REALITY

Now is the time for the Church to awaken to righteousness and "sin not."

> *Therefore, if anyone is in Christ, he is
> a new creation; old things have passed away;
> behold, all things have become new.*
> 2 CORINTHIANS 5:17

How do we make this righteousness a reality? A major player is our mouth, and we'll discuss that in greater detail in

Chapter Seven. When we begin to *speak* over us what God has *declared* over us, faith begins to rise within and redirects the course of our lives.

Another task we must complete is learning to forgive ourselves! How can we possibly hold onto a sin or failure that God has forgiven? If we think we are a better judge than He, we've been deceived.

Hell has been able to restrain and oppress the Church by sins that were placed and erased under the Blood of the Lamb years ago! We simply have not believed that the Blood is sufficient or that God really does watch over His Word to perform it.

How can we possibly hold onto a sin or failure that God has forgiven?

We have been set free, although the reality of that freedom does not come automatically. Liberty in a particular area manifests when we continually act on the truth in that realm. It takes time to remove the grave clothes that have held us in bondage, but we can shed them and soar as an eagle up in the heavenlies with Jesus!

A NEW KINGDOM

If our sins have been forgiven as the Word states, then, of course, guilt and punishment are removed. No penalty is due. We are released from the fear of God's judgment on our lives. Sin makes us afraid of God – just as Adam was in the Garden of Eden—yet He is merciful.

There is a provision to deal with sin anytime we yield to it, but we have to know, receive, and believe what our Father has already done for us through Jesus. When we fail, the Blood is still available on that Mercy Seat in Heaven to forgive and cleanse us of any unrighteousness, and restore the breach between ourselves and God.

When we were freed at the new birth, we were born into a Kingdom we knew nothing about. From that beginning we must learn how to walk in liberty, to understand how God thinks, and put these truths into practice. So, without a diligent and dedicated effort to press toward God in the Word, quite often we fall back into our old sin patterns because we are so much more familiar with our old ways.

> *Deep within our inward man, we must continually push into the things of God.*

We may love God, but we tend to withdraw and hesitate to plunge into uncharted waters. So, deep within our inward man, we must continually push into the things of God.

"DOMINION AND POWER"

With righteousness, there is a freedom in God to be, to become, and to reach new heights. Remember the definition of righteousness: it is the ability to come boldly into the presence of a Holy God without a sense of guilt, inferiority, or condemnation.

We need to allow those around us to become righteous on their own. People are afraid of freedom, especially if we are walking in it and they are not.

A word of caution: others don't usually rejoice when we begin to walk out who God says we are unless they are in lock step with us. This is sad, but true. They try to trip and set us up for failure! But greater is He Who is in us than he who is in the world!

Now to Him who is able to keep you from
stumbling, and to present you faultless before
the presence of His glory with exceeding joy,
To God our Savior,
Who alone is wise,
Be glory and majesty,
Dominion and power,
Both now and forever.
Amen.
JUDE 24-25

What a powerful proclamation. The God we serve is able to keep us from stumbling. If we have faltered in the past, it's because we have taken charge and negated His actions to keep us upright. When we walk in the flesh instead of the Spirit, we fall. Yet, because of the capacities of righteousness, He is able to keep us from stumbling in this life, and present us faultless, coming into His glory with joy! Glory to God!

UNDER OUR HEEL

Many Christians say "We will be victorious in heaven" and that is certainly true, but the devil won't be there! And we are instructed to be overcomers here on this planet! It's important that we keep the devil under our feet *here!*

As members of the Army of God, we must take action against the evil running loose so that the will of God can be done on earth as it is being done in heaven!

Life in this crazy world necessitates victory because we have an enemy that catapults resistance and turmoil from all directions. But in truth, our right-standing with God equips us with all of heaven's resources to keep the devil under our heel and realize success in the Name of Jesus! If we could only receive this truth, our lives would be much different.

IT'S YOUR CHOICE

We have been declared righteous before the courts of heaven through Jesus Christ. The Father has made provision that no person need go to hell, yet people are bursting hell wide open every day, defiant in the face of a Holy Righteous God. He did not intend for this to happen, but people make choices which regulate the course of their lives.

In the same manner, God made a way for us to live uprightly and abundantly—for our sins to be completely forgiven and erased—for us to live above the norm as we journey through this life.

Through our Lord, He has made a way to force hell to bow its knee to the voice of God's Word coming out of our mouths in the Name of Jesus! Yes, that path is established, but just because God has made it possible does not mean it is working in our lives. These things depend on our choices and our cooperation with Jehovah. We have to accept *and* follow Him as Lord and Savior.

Next, we must begin the process of developing our faith, believing what God says is available to us truly *does* belong to us. Our inheritance is in place and established, but it is *we* who must seize these gifts He offers and say, "I want it. I receive it. Thank You, Lord!"

Those of us who take the provisions of God's grace and this free gift of righteousness and pull them to our bosom are the ones who walk in abundance and in the fullness of what God has intended for His children from the beginning.

PROCLAIM AND OCCUPY

There are likely millions upon millions of Christians who know that Jesus came to "save" them from sin, but are unaware that salvation brought anything else and, therefore, are not experiencing the fullness of what He has made available for His people. Remember, God said, "My people perish for a lack of knowledge."

What we know and understand, and what choices we make are absolutely crucial! If we do not occupy and live out the provisions He has given, even though they are ours, there are those who will take squatter's rights from us and we will have to run them off.

We move forward in Christ through revelation knowledge of what God has done. Continued compliance to the truths of God's Word makes us free—accepting Him at His Word and knowing He cannot lie.

Continued compliance to the truths of God's Word makes us free!

God is completely on our side— and if He be for us who can be against us (Romans 8:31)? Yet we must proclaim, occupy, and take what God says is rightfully ours. The new birth is a free gift from above, yet we must reach out and lay claim to the gift that has been offered.

MAKE IT YOURS

It is against the will of God that any man perish and go to hell. Yet the Father doesn't *force* anyone to accept Jesus as Lord and Savior. This new birth doesn't occur just because we are hell-bound. We have to hear it, believe it, and act on the Gospel.

Healing is the same. There is provision in God's Word to walk free of sickness and disease, and that is the will of God. But healing does not occur just because our bodies are sick and dying. Nor does it manifest just because we cry buckets of tears before Almighty God. It requires our will, our choices, and our actions for *any* of God's blessings to be evidenced in our lives, even though they do belong to us.

Every ability to break hell's bondage has been given freely through righteousness, but we have to claim it and make it ours. We must hold it tightly because Satan is always trying to make us believe something other than the truth of God's Word. He doesn't want the Lord to release the victory that will surely follow.

Aren't you glad this awesome God we serve has already defeated the devil for us? Hallelujah!

> *But God, who is rich in mercy, because of His great love with which He loved us, even when we were dead in trespasses, made us alive together with Christ (by grace you have been saved), and raised us up together, and made us sit together in the heavenly places in Christ Jesus.*
>
> EPHESIANS 2:4-6

> *...and what is the exceeding greatness of His power toward us who believe, according to the working of His mighty power which He worked in Christ when He raised Him from the dead and seated Him at His right hand in the heavenly places, far above all principality and power and might and dominion, and every name that is named, not only in this age but also in that which is to come.*
>
> EPHESIANS 1:19-21

Righteousness has raised us up with Jesus in heavenly places. Think about this. If Jesus is highly exalted and He is lifted high, far above all principalities and powers and rulers of the darkness, and we are seated up there with Him, where does that put us in relation to Satan's kingdom? *Far above it!* Glory to God Almighty!

I am telling you, Church, He has done marvelous things for us! This means that all darkness is under *our* feet as well. But to enter His victory, we must become knowledgeable of the gifts He has given us at the moment of the new birth, and be transformed to think, talk, and act like Him.

That process is what I want to share with you next: sanctification, and our position in Christ.

CHAPTER 6

$\mathcal{A}$ MESS OR A MESSAGE?

$\mathcal{P}$eople are watching. They want to see if we do the right or "righteous" thing even when we think no one is looking—they are observing to determine if we live what we preach. And what they see in us greatly affects how they respond to God when the Gospel is presented to them.

Our attitudes, words, and actions are to be an extension of His love and personality. But far too frequently, our lives leave a "bad taste" in the sinner's mouth, making these individuals difficult to evangelize later.

Is our life a mess or a message to others? As people look at us, are they drawn to God or are they repelled from the Lord we represent? Frankly, we are the *only* "Bible" the world is seeing. Do they like what they are reading on the pages of our lives? Are we a good advertisement for the Kingdom of God or a deterrent?

Here's what the Bible says concerning the matter:

But when the kindness and the love of God our Savior toward man appeared, not by works of righteousness which we have done, but according to His mercy He saved us, through the washing of regeneration and renewing of the Holy Spirit, whom He poured out on us abundantly through Jesus Christ our Savior, that having been justified by His grace we should become heirs according to the hope of eternal life.

TITUS 3:4-7

...but as He who called you is holy, you also be holy in all your conduct, because it is written, "Be holy, for I am holy."

1 PETER 1:15-16

...that you put off, concerning your former conduct, the old man which grows corrupt according to the deceitful lusts, and be renewed in the spirit of your mind, and that you put on the new man which was created according to God, in true righteousness and holiness.

EPHESIANS 4:22-24

The key to Christ-like conduct is found in one word: *sanctification.*

Whereas justification and righteousness are works of God in our lives, sanctification is basically *our* responsibility. It is that process when we die more and more to self and our old ways and thoughts, and become conformed to the image of the Lord Jesus.

SET APART

Sanctification is an ongoing work that deals specifically with our character and our open and hidden lifestyle before God and others. It sets us apart from the world and its evil ways—and must occur in our lives for us to live in victory. Our old patterns of thoughts and actions are in opposition to God and, therefore, do not bring positive results in the Kingdom.

Even though we are born again, God is not free to accomplish in and through us what He desires. We must continually grow in the spirit realm and learn to "flow" with Him in order to enter the abundant, victorious life He has planned in His heart from before the beginning of time.

But of Him you are in Christ Jesus, who became for us wisdom from God – and righteousness and sanctification and redemption –

I CORINTHIANS 1:30

The moment we accept Christ eternal life is poured into us and we become filled with God Himself. His nature and His substance are imparted deep within to enable us to overcome obstacles for ourselves and others. He also empowers us to become an integral part of the Church in all of Her fullness and glory!

We are living, walking billboards, everywhere we go.

God has destined us to be that vehicle through which He is revealed to this dying world. Privileged to the wisdom of the Father through our Lord Jesus, the Church of the Living God potentially has the answer to all of the questions that plague mankind. With the Holy Spirit residing within each one of us, we are to be free-flowing carriers of God's explosive power everywhere we go—and vessels to deliver healing and liberty.

We are to represent God Almighty as we exemplify His character by extending our hands and words in compassion, grace, and mercy. In reality, we are living, walking billboards, advertising not only God Himself, but also His Kingdom's goodness.

THE UPRIGHT WALK

Sadly, the world has been harmed and disheartened by the Church and the manner in which believers have behaved. This is because so few members of the Body of Christ have gone further than the initial new birth experience. Only a small minority has endeavored to go through the sanctification process in order to live a holy and upright lifestyle before God and man.

Somehow, we have believed that attending Church and reading the Bible is enough. And although these actions are necessary and commendable, they are not enough to live a life pleasing to the Lord. Knowing what God has done through righteousness and His goodness that has abounded toward us, it should be a natural thing to keep moving toward conformity with His Son Jesus.

Realizing the great cost God paid for you and me, it should be in our hearts to endeavor to walk uprightly, pleasing to Him. And were we truly grateful for what He has obtained—enabling us to escape hell and walk free from bondage—we would be eager to make these changes.

> *Therefore we were buried with Him through baptism into death, that just as Christ was raised from the dead by the glory of the Father, even so we also should walk in newness of life. For if we have been united together in the likeness of His death, certainly we also shall be in the likeness of His resurrection, knowing this, that our old man was crucified with Him, that the body of sin might be done away with, that we should no longer be slaves of sin.*
>
> ROMANS 6:4-6

How we act and talk in front of others is extremely important. It is crucial how we respond in unpleasant situations, whether anyone is around or not. Our new birth and justification broke the power of sin over us so that we might walk in this newness of eternal life. God wants, but also *needs* us to be witnesses of the greatness of our Lord and His Kingdom to others that are not yet acquainted with Him.

WE'RE AMBASSADORS!

The message we portray is vital in light of the great commission we are commanded to fulfill—to go into all of the world and preach the Gospel and make disciples of all nations.

> *Now all things are of God, who has reconciled us to Himself through Jesus Christ, and has given us the ministry of reconciliation, that is, that God was in Christ reconciling the world to Himself, not imputing their trespasses to them, and has committed to us the word of reconciliation. Now then, we are ambassadors for Christ, as though God were pleading through us: we implore you on Christ's behalf, be reconciled to God.*
>
> 2 CORINTHIANS 5:18-20

According to these Scriptures, everyone has a ministry. We are each called to present the goodness of His Gospel to men and urge them to be reconciled with God. It is our job as representatives of the Father. God is not upset with you. He loves you and yearns for your fellowship! He knows you by name and comes to rescue you through His Son, Jesus Christ. Will you present yourself to Him so He can remove the heavy weight of sin and set you free?

What a calling! What a ministry! Yet, people will accept or reject these words based on previous experiences with "Christians" and their day to day contact with them. I am grieved that through the mouths of many sinners, I hear the words, "The Church is full of hypocrites! I don't want anything to do with God."

Our witness is absolutely essential. We need to strive to be conformed to the image of our Lord Jesus. The world is waiting on us to be the sons and daughters of God we claim to be with all the integrity, grace, and love of the Father we represent.

The world is waiting on us to be the sons and daughters of God we claim to be.

How we see ourselves will reflect in our actions and words, "for as a man thinketh in his heart, so is he" (Proverbs 23:7). We are exactly what we think we are!

OUR INVITATION

One of our greatest enemies is the sense of unworthiness. We can't really move into that next dimension with God if we are caught up in all that we did, and *should* have done.

If we continue to dwell on the things we have missed, the messes we've made, and how bad we have been, we can't really believe the Good News—much less act on it. But, according to the Word of God, if we are born again and washed in the precious Blood of Jesus, God doesn't even remember those past events! It's so wonderful what our Father has done for us! Can we dare to believe it?

We are nothing in ourselves, but in Christ Jesus we are changed and transformed into His glorious image and are given an open invitation to come to the Throne Room whenever we desire. If we could truly comprehend what He has done for us and what those actions have created us to be in His sight, our lives would be gloriously transformed.

OUR SOURCE OF SUPPLY

Do we really understand what hell has done by blanketing our thoughts and inner convictions with this "unworthy" mess? So often hell whispers in our ears about yesterday and our faults. It reminds us of events long ago eradicated by the Blood of the Lamb! Hell has the nerve to bring up things that are outright lies hoping we will accept them—and most of us do because we have not understood the work of grace in our lives. Too often, we forget what God has done for us.

This feeling of unworthiness makes us weak, holds us back, and drives us to act foolishly in front of others. Remember, our sins and sense of guilt and condemnation make us feel and act inferior, and many times *ugly*, before God and man. All this was birthed from something that in the eyes of God does not exist—our past. We must wake up to the truth of righteousness to move into the glorious realm that lies just ahead.

But whether we recognize these things or not isn't in the hands of God. How much we understand of righteousness is in *our* control and will determine how we relate to others. And I'm here to tell you, we know very little.

We must stop making people our source and supply and turn to the Lord. It's time to quit expecting from others what we are not willing to give. We need to start seeing those around us in the same light that God sees them and cease being their judge and jury.

"SUDDENLY"

Do you remember what happened at the day of Pentecost?

"Suddenly, there came a sound from heaven" (Acts 2:2). I believe a God-ordained "suddenly" of His presence is standing at the door of the Church, ready to enter. It will be wonderful. But we've got to change and begin to respond in agreement with the truths of righteousness for them to manifest on our behalf. Righteousness is received by faith even though it is given by God.

"CHEAP GRACE?"?

Why is it we want to punish ourselves over and over, year after year? Basically, religion has taught us to do just that—to blame ourselves with yesterday's sin, to beat our brow, and call ourselves unworthy. When "religion" rather than relationship is in our hearts, and we attend churches that can't accept the goodness of God, it is hard for us to believe that forgiveness can be as simple as it is.

It truly is easy to be forgiven, but let's not forget that it cost a great deal – the Blood and the life of our Lord Jesus. He died on the Cross for us.

Forgiveness is not cheap, although "cheap grace" has been taught over the

Forgiveness is not cheap, although "cheap grace" has been taught over the years.

years. In other words, we've thought it is okay to live any way we want and be forgiven in the morning. Yes, pardon can be realized, but it is an abomination for God's people to live their lives that way on purpose.

Jesus said if we love Him, we will keep His commandments. If we find ourselves desiring to live a sloppy life of sin, we need to get close to God and reassess our salvation.

The mercy and grace the Lord has for us is new every

morning and can catapult us to the next level and adventure with God!

SPIRITUAL ADULTS

We must become more *spiritually* centered than *earthly* centered; in other words, we must see ourselves more from our spiritual perspective than the natural. Though many believers have served the Lord fifty years, some are still infants who really don't know anything about spiritual things and don't see anything different in their perspective *except*

> *We must become more spiritually centered than earthly centered.*

that they are heaven bound. They are not yet feeding on the meat of the Word and even "squawk" when the preached "milk" is not to their liking! They have a hard time swallowing or digesting any spiritual truth!

Some want the Church to pamper and wait on them hand and foot, year after year, much as we would a natural baby, while God desires that each of us mature in Him and minister to the lost. We must move into the flow and challenge people to develop in the spirit realm to adulthood and give them room to do so.

Allow me to interject this thought. The government welfare system has really damaged many because the welfare mentality is not Scriptural. It was introduced in our nation to fill in a gap, but we've made it a lifestyle – even to generations! If you find yourself a recipient, thank God that such a program is available for you, but use it only as a springboard to move ahead!

Don't let your life be captured by handouts because it will hurt your walk with God. If that happens, you'll find yourself with an attitude of expecting someone to take care of everything for you.

Regrettably, the Church is falling into that deception and we must prevent it from becoming anymore prevalent than it already is.

THE CHANGE FACTOR

We are declared righteous at the moment of our new birth, but whether we utilize faith will determine if it operates in our lives or not. It is a faith walk, not a *feeling* thing. God is waiting on us to take righteousness to our bosom and do something with it, instead of being so earthly bound that we judge everything on our mood of the day.

We all act foolishly from time to time; but whether we behave like a fool or not has no bearing on being righteous. It just means we didn't walk out who we are. It indicates we are living below our high calling in Christ Jesus and it becomes apparent that we need to make additional changes.

To live within this wonderful calling requires us to be flexible, and most of us balk and resist change because it makes us uncomfortable and somewhat fearful. Since the Almighty never changes, *we must!*

YOUR IDENTITY

Instead of basing our worth on the unchangeable Word of God that is always the truth, most of us have a tendency to find our value in things that are temporal. For example, many people identify themselves to others by their job, their family, or their college education. If such things are central to how we see ourselves—if a university degree makes us somebody or gives us worth—then we are in for a hard time, because that is not who we are anymore.

In fact, these are *natural* things, and Scripture states that what we can see with our natural eye and hear with our natural ear are subject to change. If we view who we are based on the position we hold at our place of employment, all the devil would need to do is manipulate it in some way to affect us.

Satan might even try to eliminate your position, causing you to fall back into inferiority and depression because that is what made you. In your eyes, that's who you are.

No. Your job or position is what you *do*, not who you *are*. Please understand, there isn't anything wrong with what we've accomplished in the natural, but we must find our true value and worth in Christ Jesus!

What we learn to live out from the Word of God – how we walk in His glory—how much we open the door for God to live in and through us—these are the things that make us valuable.

TRANSFORMED!

God lives in us and we live in Him! We can be at any level in the spiritual or natural realm, and no matter what anyone does to us, we won't lose our value *if* we know who we are and what great things God has done in our lives. But we have to find our worth in Him. If we will do that, change will not be so upsetting to us.

Our entire walk with God is filled with transformation. Just the simple fact that God says we go from glory to glory echoes a changing glory. His Word sets the standard, and we are changed as we behold Jesus in that Word. It raises us to His excellence. Again, the Word doesn't alter, but we do. So our identity cannot be based on anything in this natural realm which is subject to corruption and decay.

Change, by its very nature, modifies what it touches, and can influence the things we think make us who we are. Yet these earthly endeavors have nothing to do with our eternal position with God—which is much more important.

Whether we have a pulpit ministry or not, the title that shines the brightest is "Child of God—born again—washed clean by the Blood of the Lamb!" That's who we are! Every time we walk into a room we bring the sweet presence of Almighty God with us! That is our value! We are spirit beings with the nature of the Lord in us and we can accomplish outstanding things through Jehovah God!

> *Every time we walk into a room we bring the sweet presence of Almighty God with us!*

GOD IS GOD!

Sometimes, we encounter people who are walking in His power and favor to such a degree that they capture more of the Lord than most. It almost seems that God has a heavier hand on them and shows them favoritism. Yet that is not true.

When certain individuals manifest the Father more than others, they have learned, taken hold of, and understood a simple principle: If God is God—then God is God! And that has elevated them to another level.

When that same truth penetrates our spirit, people will be drawn to us like a magnet, because we will start radiating Him. To evangelize this world, our lives need to be a message of God's wealth, God's health, and God's redemption, delivered with a wonderful attitude.

Wherever we are planted, we need to be releasing "a sweet aroma" of Christ (2 Corinthians 2:15-16). As we walk with the Lord, people ought to be smelling the sweet presence of God. Something about our life should draw people toward the Lord. We need to live in such a way that we entice those in darkness to come to the Light, bring hope to the hopeless, and *lift* their situation. People may not understand why, but they will want what we have!

AN INDICTMENT!

Let me repeat my question again: are we a mess or a message? Most of us have not been good advertisements for the Lord. For instance, I've talked with waiters and waitresses in restaurants who confided that the worst people to serve are the "Christians" on Sunday morning right out of Church! Our reputation is that we are demanding, rude, complaining, and stingy. How sad. And what a bad indictment on the Church as a whole.

> *Sinners view the entire Church when they look at the actions of our life.*

Remember, sinners view the entire Church when they look at the actions of our life—and rightfully so, because we are one Body. So what you do affects me, and what I do affects you—and how others respond to you. Our witness is so important!

Must of us do nothing about our "mess." Instead we talk about it and stir it up – saturating ourselves in our tangled web and don't pay the price to break free.

As a pastor, I hear repeatedly, "I can't help it!"

Is that really the truth? If we can't do something with ourselves—with Almighty God empowering us from the inside—then there is no one on the face of this earth who can! We need to point our finger at ourselves and say, "I am the problem—me and my flesh. I enjoy my flesh and I let it rule, regardless of the mess my life is in!"

You see, this is not a "God" responsibility, it's ours! The

Lord has already imparted all of the faith we will need, but it must be nurtured through the Word.

Our frame of mind will greatly determine the outcome of our efforts. Our attitudes radiate from us and create the atmosphere in which we reside. All of us at one time or another have occasionally regressed to "Mess City" when in fact we should be looking for a Holy City.

CLAIM IT!

I have a deep concern for those who hear and hear the Gospel, yet never change – those who continue in bondage and fail to come to a knowledge of the truth.

Hallelujah, there is freedom in Christ Jesus; He is the Deliverer for all men, for all times. But He doesn't just snatch us out of turmoil without our participation. We have to reach up and take hold of God's Word. He is waiting on us at some point to straighten our backbone, to be bold in Him, to step out, and believe He didn't lie when He spoke the Words in the Holy Book.

The Bible doesn't *contain* God's Word—it *is* God's Word, written in a language we can understand so that we can claim it and He can fulfill it! That is the reason the Father had the Bible written for us. He wants to see man completely delivered from the hand of the enemy and riding the high wings of victory! And the Bible tells us how this is accomplished. Praise God forevermore!

THE FAITH FACTOR

It takes the Word of God to change, mature, and usher us into victory. His Word also instructs us how to overcome the world, the flesh, and the devil. As we learn to use our faith in this Word, we begin to grasp what God has provided for us.

The answer to our problems and needs is supplied in the

spirit realm, but to be effective, it must manifest in the natural. Faith is that process whereby we take what we need out of the spirit realm and bring it into the natural realm.

God has given to each of us a measure of faith. We then take what we are given and develop it—allowing it to grow by "hearing and hearing" and participating in the Word. We allow that Word—the power of God—to come inside and abide there, conforming what Jehovah has called us to be.

For I am not ashamed of the gospel of Christ, for it is the power of God to salvation for everyone who believes, for the Jew first and also for the Greek. For in it the righteousness of God is revealed from faith to faith; as it is written, "The just shall live by faith."

ROMANS 1:16-17

The Gospel—the Good News—the Word of God *is* the power of the Almighty to bring us healing, deliverance, and to set us free from sin. We are not ashamed of the Gospel because it breaks the power of sickness, disease, and bondage that has held us captive and wipes away sin and its stain.

In the Word, the righteousness of God is revealed from faith to faith. So how do you move on from glory to glory with the Father? You simply go from faith to faith!

We don't wake up one morning with enough faith to believe everything God said in The Book. Instead, we build our faith one step at a time, taking hold of one area and then moving to another. We read a promise of God and begin to believe by speaking and acting on it until it manifests—then we move into another promise while we maintain what we have already received.

In order to be evident in our lives, the promises of God must be more real than the situations and problems around us.

In other words, the spirit world has to become more real than the natural one.

SIN-CONSCIOUS?

If all we do is think about how we've missed out – how pitiful we are—how nothing is working for us, and how bad we've been, our faith will not work. I believe being overly conscious of our sin and failures stymies our spiritual growth. When we are tuned to our own inabilities and fears and everything from which God is trying to sever us, we're staying on the negative side of life. Seeing our world through "sin-conscious glasses" habitually holds us back.

Now is the time to become righteous-conscious and begin to rejoice in what God has done for us—and who we are in Him.

Now is the time to become righteousness-conscious and begin to rejoice in what God has done for us— and who we are in Him. We need to see ourselves as the Word says we are, and relinquish our sin. We must act upon Scripture and take off the old man, putting on the new man that is created in the image of the Almighty!

God is our Helper, but He will not do this *for* us; the responsibility is ours and we can only accomplish this when we are centered in righteousness.

OUR STATEMENT

Being sin-conscious is not the same as living in sin. If the devil is unable to keep us shackled either in open or hidden sin, then he makes us sin-conscious. It keeps us tuned to our own failures, or someone else's. As I have observed, the

Church is filled with people like this.

It astounds me how many confessing, go-to-church Christians are living in open sin. They are "shacking up," living in immorality – even writing "faith" checks knowing there are insufficient funds in their accounts. They arrive continually late for work and are perpetrators of strife and gossip among their associates. They are defrauding and cheating others, lying in business transactions or on taxes, yet claiming to love the Lord. What kind of a statement are we presenting to this lost and dying world? What advertisements have we become for the Kingdom of God?

What kind of a statement are we presenting to this lost and dying world?

For the glorious Church to rise up and be heard, it is time to come alive unto righteousness and walk out of the mess we have created. Glory comes to the Body when righteousness is exalted. It is not manifest in a group of people who do not act, talk, or think as if they're righteous, even though, in reality, they are.

LINE UPON LINE!

It excites me to know that I am delivered from sin, fear, death, sickness and lack, and that this glory resides on the inside of me. I'm thrilled to know I can be different and break the cycles in my life so I can be a vessel of honor fit for the Master's use.

Be aware that God is not holding us back, but inciting us to press toward the goal of this high calling. It has always been our Father's good pleasure to give us the Kingdom. He has already deposited in us what we need to climb up out of our man-made mess and be the message of hope to others!

Walking in righteousness takes stamina of spirit and faith in God. Our battle, however, is consumed with dealing in doubt because we live in a world that absolutely tries to blow holes in the truth of the Word every day. Unregenerate men strive to discredit and disprove the Scriptures as they make fun of the Gospel of Jesus Christ.

The world has some crazy ideas about God because they don't know Him. Everyday they endeavor to prove that the Father is not Who He said He is and that He did not do what the Book declares He's already done for us.

You and I grow in faith as we begin to believe and trust in God, line upon line, precept upon precept, here a little, there a little (Isaiah 28:10). When we genuinely believe that through God this Bible was written as the present day message of the Lord to us—and that these Words are His directions for success—we move forward.

As we take what He has written, believe and apply it to our lives in power, we then begin to experience miraculous results.

IT'S COMPLETED!

This fabulous, abundant life is there for us—it is already ours, paid for by the precious Blood of the Lamb! How wonderful it can be to receive everything God says is true! His love and mercy are so far-reaching and endless they are hard to grasp in a real way because we have never before experienced perfect love. It is difficult to fathom the greatness of this life that God has so freely given us, yet it is ours just the same. If we are not experiencing this life day after day, it is not His fault, but ours alone.

But this Man [Jesus], after He had offered
one sacrifice for sins forever, sat down at the right

hand of God, from that time waiting till His
enemies are made His footstool.

HEBREWS 10:12-13

The work of the Lord Jesus has been completed. The devil is a liar, a loser and has already been defeated—Jesus has paid the price for our deliverance. In fact, He's done all He is going to do pertaining to the devil in our lives, just as He has completed everything He's planned for our healing, freedom, and salvation. It's now our responsibility to find out what He has already accomplished and then take it, believe it, and walk in it.

Jesus' work is finished and He is sitting down next to the Father waiting for His enemies to be made His footstool. Knowing we are a part of the Body of Christ and that the "foot" is in the Body, it is our task to place the devil under our feet! And it is totally attainable by taking the Word of God and His Name and slamming it in the devil's face!

Too often, we accuse others and even point our spiritual artillery toward heaven itself to account for why things aren't working in our lives, but the blame rests with us!

LIVE THE WORD

With our inheritance already "probated" in Heaven's courts after the death and resurrection of the Lord Jesus, God is waiting on us to enter into and walk in this newness of life. Surprisingly, He will not force us to become who He has destined us to be.

Even if we have taken the time to memorize scriptures, if they are not working for us, then we are just basically in mental assent with them—only agreeing in our head; we are not in faith. If they are not showing forth in our daily lives, we don't have revelation of the Word that will set us free.

When we "take" scriptures and make them ours, we live in them. In so doing we conform our actions, and perhaps even break bad habits. Yes, it takes effort and conscious thought until it becomes natural for us. For instance, we must resist our fleshly desire to become angry with others and, instead, demonstrate the love of God.

We may know what to do and *not* walk it in our daily life, but if that is the case, the scriptures have not yet taken root within us.

ARE YOU REIGNING?

Often, we are so eager to serve that we forget to reign. Real service for God comes out of reigning with Him. As a born again believer you have a new position in Christ, far above principalities and powers.

God wants us to reign over ourselves and our circumstances, and then serve out of that status—as did His Son. When we serve without reigning, we are in a works mentality. Jesus could become a servant because He knew Who He was—and how to receive from God.

Many believers remain only on the giving end, not knowing they are to accept what God offers. When that happens, they are only partially participating in what God has done for them.

If we can't receive from people around us, I promise you, we will struggle to receive from God. We'll see things in the Word and will admire them—talk about and desire to have them—yet will have a difficult time walking in His glory because we don't know how to receive.

Low self image is why most of us wrestle with this problem, whether it be receiving from people or God Himself. We just basically hope the Lord will hear our prayers, because we haven't learned how to reign.

101

TAKE OFF YOUR GRAVE CLOTHES.

Reigning involves both giving and taking. For example, we rejoice in what God has done for us, but most of the Church world goes no further. Let me say it this way: many believers are still parked at Calvary and haven't been resurrected from the grave! We have not risen to take our seats next to Him in heavenly places.

And you He made alive, who were dead in trespasses and sins, in which you once walked according to the course of this world, according to the prince of the power of the air, the spirit who now works in the sons of disobedience, among whom also we all once conducted ourselves in the lusts of our flesh, fulfilling the desires of the flesh and of the mind, and were by nature children of wrath, just as the others. But God, who is rich in mercy, because of His great love with which He loved us, even when we were dead in trespasses, made us alive together with Christ (by grace you have been saved), and raised us up together, and made us sit together in the heavenly places in Christ Jesus.

EPHESIANS 2:1-6

There it is! According to God's Word we are positionally seated with Jesus in heavenly places to rule and reign as His ambassadors, despite our former sins and failures. He dealt with our past through the Cross of Calvary because He wanted us lifted high with Him! Glory!

However, if we remain at Calvary, still talking about death but never allowing death to take place in us, how can He resurrect us to this newness of life? We have not gone beyond the grave and turned loose of yesterday. If we haven't

102

laid our grave clothes down and left them obliterated under the Blood where they belong, we can't ascend to sit and reign with Him from that heavenly realm. It is those grave clothes that keep our life a mess of confusion instead of a message of honor!

From our position seated with Jesus in heavenly places, do you understand that we have to look *down* to reign? We can only go so far in this abundant life if we remain centered on the Cross. I am not speaking against the Cross because without it there would be no salvation.

We must lay down our grave clothes and put on our robes of righteousness.

Certainly, many men died on a cross who were neither holy nor righteous. Had Jesus not risen from that grave, triumphant over death, the Cross would have accomplished very little! So, if all we see of our redemption is what happened at Calvary, we stay, in a sense, "dead."

The truth is, we have been raised from death to walk in this resurrection life that Jesus purchased for us! We have been brought to new life by the glory of the Father to be mobile, shining messages of hope to this dying world. But we must lay down our grave clothes and put on our robes of righteousness—making a choice to begin our journey upward to victory with God!

AVAILING PRAYER

Of course, it takes effort to move forward toward conformity with Jesus. We have to step into a new realm and break out of the cycles that have constrained us. To really walk in the fullness of our Christianity, we must learn to be risk takers and become determined enough to push through barriers. We can't just sit back on Cushion Street, making no changes, and expecting things to flourish.

God encourages us to step out of our past and lay hold of our future. The greatest adventure of our life begins with God! And He responds to our prayer.

> *Confess your trespasses to one another, and pray for one another, that you may be healed. The effective, fervent prayer of a righteous man avails much.*
>
> JAMES 5:16

The availing prayer of a righteous, sanctified saint is answered! But this elite group is not comprised of those who have just "heard" that they are righteous, rather people who understand what it has accomplished for them.

Again, righteousness does not work just because we are special in the eyes of God. We are able to carry out great things in this earth for the Kingdom because we *know* our sins are forgiven—we *know* our rights and privileges—and we *know* how to rule and reign while we remain submitted unto God.

We can't just say that "the prayers of a righteous man avail much" and expect it to work when we are weaklings, walking in condemnation and guilt, and feeling so inferior we can't even hold up our head. That's a deception. All of those things run counter to living a victorious life in our Lord Jesus.

"RIGHT LIVING"

We should not be concerned whether the world is walking in righteousness, but rather if they are headed for hell. Obviously, we cannot go to the four corners of the earth and start by teaching "right living" when they aren't even born again. We can't judge, nor be surprised that they are living in blatant sin—they are serving the devil whether they know it or not. It's the Church that we first have to be concerned with; we, as believers, are supposed to know better. Remember, we are walking billboards, advertising God and His Kingdom everywhere we go.

There ought to be such an obvious difference between Christians and the world, in attitudes, actions, victory, and love that they become jealous of what we have. Unbelievers should run with great anticipation to the House of God to find out what it is we possess!

Let us be The Triumphant Body of Christ walking in her fullness. Glory days are just ahead for those who are ready to move ahead. Determine to embrace this wonderful gift of righteousness and wear your robe with honor and humility— to reign in this life by the one Man, Jesus Christ.

May you take your rightful place with Jesus in heavenly places to the glory of God the Father!

CHAPTER 7

*D*ECLARE, DECREE, AFFIRM!

*W*ords are powerful weapons. With them we can announce and confirm what will take place in our lives, our families, and our nation. It is with words that we place the devil under subjection and keep him there.

Unfortunately, few of us comprehend the gravity of what falls from our mouth all too freely. We don't take our own words seriously. This is apparent since we speak, without thought, curses on ourselves and others—even while laughing. We literally have no idea what havoc we are creating by the evil things we verbalize.

But the righteousness of faith speaks in this way, "Do not say in your heart, 'Who will ascend into heaven?'" (that is, to bring Christ down from above) or, "'Who will descend into the abyss?'" (that is, to bring Christ up from the dead). But what does it say? "The word is near you, in your mouth and in your heart" (that is, the word of faith which we preach): that if you confess with your mouth the Lord Jesus and believe in your heart that God has raised Him from the dead, you will

be saved. For with the heart one believes unto righteousness,
and with the mouth confession is made unto salvation.

ROMANS 10:6-10

We have already established that through the shed Blood of Jesus on Calvary, God broke the power of sin in our lives and abolished our past. He made it possible for those of us who accept Jesus as our Lord and Savior to be cleansed from the filth and weight of sin that sentenced us to death and separated us from the Father Who loved us. He sent Jesus to become sin that we might be made the righteousness of God in Him.

The shed Blood on Calvary and the resurrection of our Lord enabled God to declare each of His family members righteous and able to be partakers of the inheritance of the saints who walk in light (Ephesians 1).

Notice the question that is asked: "What does righteousness which is of faith say?" Obviously, both faith and righteousness speak—they utter words.

IT'S NEAR US

Does righteousness, which is of faith, say that Jesus has to come to earth and defeat the devil again to bring us victory? Does it declare that Jesus has to return from heaven and touch us to heal our bodies? No. Righteousness which is established in faith says that the Word of faith is near us—it's in our mouth and in our heart. And that's enough to bring about salvation in any area we have a need.

I want to remind you that "saved" does not just mean the new birth, although we have whittled it down to mean that in most churches. The new birth is wonderful and important, yet it is only the first step; it opens the door for us to receive so much more!

107

The word "saved" is the Greek word "sozo" and it means soundness, wholeness, restoration, and deliverance from temporal evils to include sickness and disease! Talk about a deal with benefits! Our salvation encompasses every area of the abundant life of God—not just the forgiveness of sin. Praise His Name!

SPEAK THE WORD!

Notice what righteousness of faith says. It declares that Jesus does not have to defeat hell again. He doesn't have to come down from heaven to do anything for us. His work has been completed and He is seated next to the Father until His enemies have been made His footstool.

We must say it until we believe it!

The Word of faith is *here*—in our mouth and in our heart. And it will establish the work in our lives that Jesus has accomplished! We use these scriptures in Romans to evangelize and bring people to the Throne of Grace, but this is an absolute principle that operates throughout the Kingdom.

Righteousness, which is of faith, simply speaks and believes the Words of faith which have been given to us by grace in the book we call the Bible.

Here is the process in a nutshell: We speak God's Word until it penetrates our hearts, not just our heads. And sometimes, to be honest, we have to speak it for a long time before we'll even start to believe it. Just because we declare the Word or memorize scripture does not mean we believe it in our hearts. Although both of these actions are good and necessary, neither even infers that we believe the Word at all. We must say it *until* we believe it.

When that Word finally drops in our heart, faith comes, and we believe *unto* our benefits of righteousness. In other words, we know what God says belongs to us because we are righteous in His eyes. Then, as that Word continues to flow out of our mouth in faith, its confession brings forth the salvation.

LIKE A RUDDER!

The book of Proverbs is packed with wisdom concerning our tongue, and I admonish you to read it, but let's take a look at the book of James. It contains one of the most revealing passages of scripture on the power of our tongue.

> *My brethren, let not many of you become teachers, knowing that we shall receive a stricter judgment. For we all stumble in many things. If anyone does not stumble in word, he is a perfect man, able also to bridle the whole body. Indeed, we put bits in horses' mouths that they may obey us, and we turn their whole body. Look also at ships: although they are so large and are driven by fierce winds, they are turned by a very small rudder wherever the pilot desires. Even so the tongue is a little member and boasts great things. See how great a forest a little fire kindles! And the tongue is a fire, a world of iniquity. The tongue is so set among our members that it defiles the whole body, and sets on fire the course of nature; and it is set on fire by hell.*
>
> JAMES 3:1-6

Wow! Our tongue can defile our entire body! It sets the course of our life in motion—good or bad. James compares our tongue to the rudder on a ship, and although it's a little member of our body, it can completely direct our life! Our tongue can kindle the flames of hellish events if we do not take it under control.

Let me clearly say that if our life is in a mess, it's because of what we have confessed with our mouth and believed in our heart as we read earlier in Romans 10. If we don't like where our life is headed, as with a ship, we must first put pressure on the rudder of our tongue! Eventually, if held steady, it will turn the course of our lives! And yet, as important as the tongue is, the decision of what is spoken lies in the heart. Jesus, Himself, said that out of the abundance of our heart, our mouth speaks (Matthew 12:34).

What is in our heart in abundance? We can determine the contents by listening to the words that flow from our mouth because it is the release valve. Our mouth is the vehicle through which our inner being speaks. It says what our heart believes and we will get exactly what we say, just like the rudder steers the ship toward its ultimate destination!

SPOKEN INTO EXISTENCE

Our words guide and direct our lives. Too often, however, instead of speaking the unchangeable truths of God which would lead our life toward glory, we declare our problems and the evil that tries and tempts us everyday. We says things such as "I guess this will fall apart," or "You know what happens, every time we plan a vacation, the kids get sick." What about: "I just can't remember anything anymore! I must be getting Alzheimer's—ha ha!"

When we utter such phrases, we are putting them in motion—we're saying this is okay; this is what we want. The more we talk about problems—how worn out we are, how broke we are, how depressed we feel, how life is not getting any better—the more we are declaring, decreeing, and affirming that we believe those things. We are confessing them out of our mouth and they are established.

Our words propel us on the road we will walk in days ahead. We can sit in church and shout "Amen!" all day long —even own fifty Bibles and thirty five notebooks crammed full of the truths on righteousness—but unless we bridle our tongue, we will remain on paths we do not want to travel.

What we really believe and speak is what we will become. That is why it is so important to begin declaring God's Word until we totally accept what He says about us is truth. His Word is *always* the truth, and that is what we want established in our lives!

↜

Victory! Peace! Joy! Health! We will never live in triumph until we begin to believe and agree with His Word. For instance, He declares that we are the head and not the tail. We may feel like the tail, and it may even *look* like we're the tail, but that is not

We will never live in triumph until we begin to believe and agree with His Word.

the truth of the matter. He said we are the head and God does not lie!

IT'S THE TRUTH!

We need to declare—and believe—that we are, indeed, who Jehovah says we are, regardless of what is going on around us! We are above and not beneath; more than conquerors. And if God be for us, who can be against us?

It's time we confess the eternal truths of the Father over ourselves, our families, and our nation. We are who God *says* we are – and can do whatever He declares we can do!

You may ask, "How can I say such things when my life is in such a mess? Am I a hypocrite when I say I am healed by the stripes of Jesus and my body is noticeably sick?" Absolutely not!

*But the wisdom that is from above [the Word
of God] is first pure, then peaceable, gentle, willing
to yield, full of mercy and good fruits, without
partiality and without hypocrisy. [insert mine]*

JAMES 3:17

The reason we can declare, decree, and affirm God's Word over us is because it is pure and without hypocrisy. We are simply stating the truth of what God has *already* spoken over us!

A hypocrite is someone who pretends to be what he is not —someone who doesn't live what he or she preaches. But if the Lord says we are *one way* and we are speaking and acting contrary to the truths God has already declared over us, are we not as guilty? The Lord has done some absolutely outstanding things for us, and yet, our words are strong against His truths, implying they are lies. No, He is true though every man is a liar (Romans 3:4).

WORDS OF INTEGRITY

Deceit is a prevalent problem within the walls of the Church. Saints who are not truthful are not only unreliable, they are dishonorable witnesses of the Lord Jesus. If we constantly lie—and that may not be blatant boldface lies but merely just stretching the truth,—we will have a very difficult time walking in faith because faith comes by hearing. That includes listening to what our mouth speaks.

Sadly, there are some chronic liars who cannot believe their own words. No wonder they have difficulty believing God. Truthfulness is vital to our integrity, which, in turn, is paramount to exhibiting righteousness. If you have not been a person of integrity, I can assure that you will have had great trouble believing God can do anything.

When we truly know the Lord, we become people of high standards and character. We are not considered trustworthy or honest if we do not fulfill what we declare. My friend, it's a lie when we put our word on the line and don't perform or follow through—from the least to our greatest promise.

God is not a man that He should lie; and because His nature was planted in us, the more we know Him, the more we should act like Him. Jesus Himself announced that Satan is the father of all lies. We cannot declare the falsehoods of the devil and consider ourselves holy and righteous before God or man.

Christians should be above reproach with character that is becoming to Almighty God.

Christians should be above reproach with character that is becoming to Almighty God. Above all, we should be a people whose word can be trusted!

DON'T HARM GOD'S TREASURE

When we lie, we heap trouble on ourselves which is not of the devil's doing. Speaking untruth pours water on our conscience and it becomes foggy. It distorts right and wrong in our minds making it almost impossible to differentiate the truth from falsehood. Where there should be black and white, there is a gray haze.

We must not affirm or repeat the lies Satan hurls at us. Hell says we are not going to change—that we are worthless, stupid fools who will never succeed at anything. The devil whispers that we're really not important to the Kingdom of God because we lived such horrendous lives before our new birth.

Nothing could be further from the truth! Every child of

God is a fragrant rose in His garden! Each of us is a treasure and extremely valuable in His sight!

What a great price was paid to retrieve us from the hand of the enemy just so we could be near our Wonderful Savior! Yet, I hear people all over the Church agreeing with those suggestions from hell! I even hear parents criticize their children and tell them over and over they will never be any good—that they will never amount to anything!

You, my friend, who call yourself God's, are a volcano of Satan's eruption on your children. You are cursing them with your mouth and bringing yourself future heartache, because they will become what you speak!

SPEAK TO THE MOUNTAIN!

God tells us continually in His Word that if we will simply *believe* what has been written down for us—getting past the whispering of every imp and demon—and begin to live day to day based on those Words from God, righteousness will exalt and raise us to a higher life!

We are not too old to change and come into agreement with the Father! His Word, spoken and believed, will "*life*" us. It will alter our entire countenance and how we deal with our family and friends. It can even transform our expectancy toward life itself. Our righteous position with Almighty God will dictate our actions, words, and thoughts.

> *For assuredly, I say to you, whoever says to this mountain, "Be removed and be cast into the sea," and does not doubt in his heart, but believes that those things he says will be done, he will have whatever he says.*
> MARK 11:23

A mountain is simply a problem or an obstacle in our life;

114

a situation that is not going according to God's Word. What does Jesus say our course of action must be? We have to speak words to it!—to command the obstruction to be removed and cast into the sea!

The Bible doesn't tell us we are to pray to the Almighty to get rid of the mountain, nor does it say we are to ask our Pastor to speak to the mountain. It's *our* mountain, our problem, and we have to do the talking!

DECREE IT!

Jesus, Himself, assures us that if we speak it with our mouth and believe it in our heart, we will have whatever we declare! Glory to God! That's why I am asking you to decree what God has spoken—not what the situation looks like.

It doesn't matter how gigantic the problem is, it will yield to our words! This principle, on the other hand, works in the negative direction just as effectively. For instance, we say, "We will never get out of this debt, every month we get deeper and deeper toward bankruptcy! I don't see how we will ever get these bills paid off!"

By saying these words, the same principle of speaking and believing that could get us out of debt completely will insure that this mountain of debt will not only remain, but multiply. It is simply because that's what we are believing and speaking over the problem!

We *believe* that we are suffering insurmountable debt, and it's getting worse. Indeed, we might be in debt up to our eyeballs, but declaring it is no road to recovery! Jesus said we will have exactly what we say. And James writes that if we want to change the course of our life, we must apply pressure to the rudder of our tongue! We must speak what we desire to happen.

WORDS OF VICTORY!

God sees the end as well as the beginning, and if we have His nature in us, we must talk in terms of the end result, which is never destruction! It is always blessing, success, and victory!

We may be seeing devastation with our natural eyes but that is not the final outcome (and it is certainly not what we desire)—unless we continue to speak those destructive words over the situation.

Our mouth is what keeps us headed in the right direction.

You might think, "How can we declare what God says when it certainly doesn't look that way?" Yet the same thing happens when we travel. We can be going from Augusta to Atlanta, Georgia, and ride on roads through towns that don't *look* anything like Atlanta, yet we keep heading toward our final destination. To be sure, Atlanta is nothing like the communities through which we travel to get there.

Just the same way, our life goals can be as different as night and day from the paths we take on the journey. And we will reach our desired objective if we keep confessing the end result and keep our mind locked on what we yearn for—not on what we can see with these natural eyes. It is our *mouth* that keeps us headed in the right direction.

Again, we become what we believe and speak. And it is not just the words we utter in church or around the pastor! It's what we say day after day in the privacy of our home.

"BEING REAL!"

I am amazed at the number of born again, Holy Ghost filled, tongue-talking Christians who stay in agreement with hell's lies and speak those curses without hesitation. Many even know about the power of the tongue and yet say when challenged on these statements, "I'm being honest. I am just being real!"

Yes, when we talk like that, we are being *real* – carnally minded! That's not walking in the Spirit, and I assure you there is no peace in speaking the devil's lies over our life (Romans 8:6). We say, "I'm just telling it like it is." No, we are telling it the way we accept it—expressing what truth is to us, and how we see ourselves.

Oh, what joy awaits when we walk, talk, and act in line with the Word of God! Let's lay down this *low life* and reach for this higher, exalted abundant life and rule and reign with God's blessing! His Word will elevate us to new dimensions, new victories, and new wonders!

Friend, we simply must change our behavior and expressions. If we stay centered on the things of this earth—on our aches, pains, and the trials of life—we will become depressed, because life without God saps our spirit.

Even more, when we are in opposition to the Father and become strangers to the covenant of promise, we are basically without hope and God is not working in our lives (Ephesians 2:12).

We need to begin saying, "This is what is happening, *but God....*" Or, "Yes, I know it looks bad, but God's Word says...." The moment we speak these words we start bringing life to a situation—for His Words are spirit and they are life. Faith is in our mouth!

CREATIVE POWER

Dear friend, we are not attempting to twist God's arm for Him to bless us, or coerce Him to declare that we are healed. He's *already* favored us with every spiritual blessing in heavenly places! We're already a privileged people and healing belongs to us. We just have to "take it" with our words.

When our mouth is full of God's promises it is much like a hydraulic pump. It is a force that surrounds and latches onto the problem, takes hold of the burden, kicks it loose, and moves it out of the way!

Since we are made in the image of God, our words contain creative power. Recognize the fact that we are the only ones in all of God's creation given the privilege and honor of speaking His Word, of governing evil, and establishing the will of God on earth as it is done in heaven! His love is unsearchable! Thank You, Lord!

God's Word is God's Word, whether it comes out of our mouth or His. When it is confessed with our lips and believed in our heart it is still the sword of the Spirit—alive and full of power.

The Father not only gave His Word to us, He put His faith in it, wrote it down, and commands us to speak it so we can be conformed to the image of His Son and defeat the devil time after time! Praise God for what righteousness has done!

We declare our faith every time we speak, and each time we pray.

> *... The effective, fervent prayer of*
> *a righteous man avails much.*
> JAMES 5:16

This verse, as translated in The Message Bible, reads: "The prayer of a person living right with God is something powerful to be reckoned with."

Those of us who know who we are can say *Glory*!

Some complain, "I don't feel like my prayers get above my nose!" Friend, they don't have to! The Holy Spirit lives *within* you! Don't base anything on how you feel. Our emotions are in the natural realm and therefore subject to the devil's influence—not to mention they are temporal and subject to change frequently.

BEYOND FEELINGS

The moment we don't sense God's presence is the time we should start confessing in faith: "Lord, I know You are here. You said You would never leave me nor forsake me. You are my Shield and Buckler. You are My God and in You do I trust!"

Our emotions are in the natural realm and therefore subject to the devil's influence.

We can never change a situation by speaking what it "looks" like or saying how we "feel" about it. We change it in the positive direction by speaking God's Words over it *until* it yields. The natural realm will always bow to the Kingdom of God *if* God's Words are declared, decreed, and affirmed long enough, regardless of our feelings.

Our bodies can be riddled with sickness and pain in the natural, but that is not the truth according to the Word. Sickness is merely a fact, and although some of it is powerful enough to kill our bodies, truth is higher and exalted, more powerful than facts!

The truth, backed up by the Blood of Jesus, is that He sent His Word, healed and delivered us from our destruction, and by His stripes we were healed (Psalms 107:20; 1 Peter 2:24). So, we keep declaring the truths of health until they become real in our heart. Healing then works its way outward and the sickness departs because life is stronger than death. Once again, righteousness is exalted! Confessing with our mouth and believing in our heart is the process—and our mouth is the key.

THE WORD WORKS!

Unfortunately, we often think we are believing the Word, yet it is only head knowledge. When it seems as though the Word is not working, we have to stop right there and remind ourselves that the Word *does* work, every time! We must point the finger at ourselves; there is no problem with God the Father, God the Word, or God the Holy Ghost. That, my friend, leaves us holding the bag!

There is a vast difference between head knowledge and heart revelation! When things get tough, the head doesn't stay with the program. If we are not watchful, it will always start to contradict and back off from the Word. On the other hand, truth, having taken root in our spirit, is anchored in the integrity of God.

We must keep speaking and meditating on those words until we can "see" it down deep within us, as clearly as our natural eye is reading this book.

AUTHORITY OVER SICKNESS

This has enormous importance for our healing.

We need to view ourselves separate from the house (body) we live in. Our spirit has been declared righteous by Almighty God and created in His image. That is the *real* man who lives in this physical body. You see, the body is not the man. If we can make a distinction between the real man that is within and the house wherein he resides, it gives us more leverage to speak to our "house" as if it were not us. We are then able to step out and command our dwelling place to line up with the Word of God and receive its healing.

By being able to separate what we see in the mirror with

who we really are, it's easier to take authority over sickness and disease and control our body. All of this is accomplished by the Word of God coming out of our mouth in faith.

ACKNOWLEDGE AND PROCLAIM

The power of our tongue is hard to grasp because we have not seen the correlation between our words and the events in our lives. That is why I have taught for many years on the importance of speaking aloud and declaring, decreeing, and affirming the right words. I've preached it again and again, yet still meet people every day who have not yet caught the message. They can quote the Scriptures. They say, "I know it says that, *but ...*"

Any time we speak the truth and add a "but," forget it! We are in unbelief! Is that plain enough?

The church I pastor hosts Healing Explosions frequently to instruct those plagued with sickness and disease on how to receive their healing—basically pleading God's case. I tell them over and over, "You have to take healing with your mouth!" And most of the time I watch the people say nothing.

Many just stare at me and keep their lips sealed, yet, I am instructing them step 1, step 2, step 3. I tell them:

- "Please open your mouth and proclaim your healing."
- "Please declare the goodness of God."
- "Please acknowledge that God won't lie."
- "Please remember God is in the healing business."
- "Agree with God no matter what is going on around you."
- "Regardless of what it feels like, speak out your healing."

121

I am amazed when no one says a word.

Our spirit needs to hear our mouth proclaim the truths of God *out loud*! We cannot be tight-lipped Christians! We must declare with our mouth the righteousness of God until it rises up in fury against those hellish things that have lodged against us!

Stand up and say, "But God....But God..." You are who Jehovah says you are!

WHAT PROBLEM?

A word of wisdom: if sickness attacks your body, don't tell people you are not ill when they can see you are as sick as a dog! You look foolish! Just say, "In the natural, this does not look very good, but I believe I receive my healing—I believe the Bible. God will turn this thing around! I am the healed of God!"

Can you imagine what the doctor must be thinking?

I've heard of people walking into the doctor's office and when the physician asks what the problem is, they reply, "I have no problem. I'm healed."

Can you imagine what the doctor must be thinking?

Listen, if you have an appointment with a physician, tell him honestly what your symptoms are and let him make a diagnosis. That way you will be able to speak to the infirmity accurately with the Word. Thank God for the medical profession; we're certainly not against physicians. If we need a doctor, we should go.

Frankly, in the area of healing, the medical profession is often working closer with God than some churches! The bottom line is that the Father wants us well; but it is to our advantage to use wisdom.

AUTHENTIC LIVING

Any situation can be turned around, yet it will change only to the degree we speak God's Word instead of the problems of life. Believing in the integrity of the Almighty must become our lifestyle. There is no need to pray for a great move in the corporate Church until we can believe for a miracle in our own home! We can't be a "faith man" in the House of God when we are not one around our own family. When we behave in such a manner we're not genuine, we are fake!

When something is real to us, we are the same whether we are at work, home, church, or on the golf course! The faith talk and faith walk should be just a natural part of who we are. When others invite us to a party, they already *know* what we are like, and apparently don't mind that Jesus is Lord of our life. However, the problem with most of the Church is that others do not see Him in our lives—and are not expecting Him to be with us. When we become one with the Lord, that's when great power will begin to flow.

Declaring God's Word will absolutely transform our lives into a higher state of glory than we ever thought possible! Sometimes, the change is so extensive, it is hard to recognize ourselves! But, that's what we yearn for, isn't it?—less of us and more of Him.

I can't emphasize this enough: the process starts with our mouth. We will either establish our problem more securely or enter into God's victory by the words we choose to speak. When we continually "declare" the issue, faith for that problem comes and increases because we are hearing it and hearing it and hearing it.

THE FIRE!

If we could see, as James 3 declares, that the words of our

123

mouth truly are kindling to every "fire" in our lives, we would be much more careful of the words we speak. We have a choice; we can have the fire of hell in our home, or we can experience the fire of the Holy Ghost within its walls!

The course of our life is set in motion by our tongue—the rudder of the ship of our life!

We will not ever have more than we declare and affirm, so it is imperative that we decree the *right* things.

If our words are divided and we say one thing at our kitchen table, another in the car, and something totally different at church to impress a fellow-believer, we are traveling down a losing highway!

My friend, if we are going to talk unbelief in our home (and *anything* that contradicts God's Word *is* unbelief), then we might as well converse that way in the sanctuary, because we *are* the Church! We are carriers of the presence of Almighty God everywhere we go!

A TREMENDOUS POWER!

Religion has us confused. It may sound good, but can make us miss every thing about God. If the sanctuary is the only place we speak faith, then we're just religious. And, if we only guard our words in front of the pastor, then this walk of righteousness is not real to us. Until we begin to speak consistently, always being the same, we will experience little victory!

We are talking about a lifestyle, yet most churches don't talk about *living out* Christianity. We must make up our minds. Are we willing to change in order to triumph?

I don't claim to understand all that is presently happening on the world scene, but I can tell you that Christ is our only salvation. Every community and nation needs to see multitudes of believers who truly are Christ-like. If we will come together and demonstrate who we are in Jesus, hell will shake. Why? Because those who are living right before God are a tremendous power to be reckoned with! We are moving into a time when the words of our mouth will either make us or break us!

When we agree with God, it gives Him something to work with. He will never concur with us that we are losers, defeated, or in bondage since in His eyes—because of the Cross and the resurrection—we are not.

When we agree with God, it gives Him something to work with.

Hell and heaven both are waiting and listening to hear what we have to say. Our words are that important! They can open the door for the devil to *legally* wreak havoc in our lives, or commission the angels of God to bring deliverance and peace.

RISE UP!

For years, I have earnestly prayed for the Church to be the Church in all of her glory and power! I've so longed to see the Body of Christ rise up to the honor of Almighty God!

Our cities need to see legions of people who are serious with God and sincerely walking in His grace and integrity before all men. This comes by understanding righteousness; allowing all the Father has deposited in us through the new birth to be a reality in us day after day.

How do we begin to show forth His glory and His brightness? By living righteously – doing and saying what is right—acting on what is honorable, even in troublesome times.

Yes, bad things happen to good people, but knowing the power of our words, let's not ever accept evil reports as a normal part of life anymore! Instead, may we take up the sword of the Spirit and the full armor of God, hitting those giants square between the eyes—making the devil crawl in the dust of the earth under our feet, where he was told to be!

When trouble strikes, Christians should really excel because we have the answer available to us through our Lord Jesus Christ, and the power of our words will overcome whatever hell throws our way!

Declare, decree and affirm it! That's what righteous living makes possible.

CHAPTER 8

*Y*IELDING TO R*IGHTEOUSNESS

*O*ne of my favorite chapters in the New Testament is Romans 6. In the letter of the Apostle Paul to the believers at Rome, he ties together many of the great themes of Christianity—sin, grace, salvation baptism, death, resurrection, righteousness and eternal life.

Let's look at these God-inspired words:

> *What shall we say then? Shall we continue*
> *in sin that grace may abound? Certainly not!*
> *How shall we who died to sin live any longer in*
> *it? Or do you not know that as many of us as were*
> *baptized into Christ Jesus were baptized into His death?*
> *Therefore we were buried with Him through baptism into*
> *death, that just as Christ was raised from the dead by the*
> *glory of the Father, even so we also should walk in*
> *newness of life. For if we have been united together*
> *in the likeness of His death, certainly we also shall*
> *be in the likeness of His resurrection, knowing*
> *this, that our old man was crucified with Him,*
> *that the body of sin might be done away with,*

that we should no longer be slaves of sin. For
he who has died has been freed from sin.

ROMANS 6:1-7

What a glorious declaration! We've been delivered from the power of sin—justified by the Blood of the Lamb and declared righteous in the eyes of Almighty God. As a result of this miraculous new birth into God's family, we have more power over our lives than Satan exhibited over us while we were yet serving darkness.

WHAT A MIRACLE!

Our righteousness in Christ Jesus is stronger than the death that held us captive with no hope of escape! But, thank God, Jesus came for us. We truly have been set free to live for our dear Savior!

> *Our righteousness in Christ Jesus is stronger than the death that held us captive.*

Sin held complete dominion over us until we were born again. At that moment, our old, unregenerate man died—it was crucified with Christ at Calvary. Jesus hung on the Cross in our place as our Substitute, and we were immersed into Him and buried through baptism into His death.

In the eyes of God, we died on Golgotha with His Son so that we might be free from sin. Yet, Jehovah didn't leave us dead! We have been resurrected to walk with God in this newness of life. The same life that raised Jesus from the dead is the power that raised us from our death!

What a miracle! God indwelled us with His own life and seated us in heavenly places beside Him!

Knowing our *old man* is dead, this newness of life enables us to be free from the dominion of sin and our fleshly nature. We were crucified with Him so that sin could be broken and we could be married or joined to another, even to Him Who is raised from the dead, to bear fruit for God (Romans 7:4).

This divine life of the Almighty gives us the power to subdue and mortify the deeds of our body and make it obey our new spirit, created in righteousness and true holiness.

"RAISED FROM THE DEAD"

The Bible declares He who has died has been liberated from sin, with all its power and control. Death no longer has a hold on us. Yes, we'll lay this body down one day, but there is no longer any *sting* in that death! Glory to God!

> *Now if we died with Christ, we believe that we shall also live with Him, knowing that Christ, having been raised from the dead, dies no more. Death no longer has dominion over Him. For the death that He died, He died to sin once for all; but the life that He lives, He lives to God. Likewise you also, reckon yourselves to be dead indeed to sin, but alive to God in Christ Jesus our Lord. Therefore do not let sin reign in your mortal body, that you should obey it in its lusts. And do not present your members as instruments of unrighteousness to sin, but present yourselves to God as being alive from the dead, and your members as instruments of righteousness to God.*
>
> ROMANS 6:8-13

> *For sin shall not have dominion over you, for you are not under law but under grace. What then? Shall we sin because we are not under law*

but under grace? Certainly not! Do you not know that to whom you present yourselves slaves to obey, you are that one's slaves whom you obey, whether of sin leading to death, or of obedience leading to righteousness? But God be thanked that though you were slaves of sin, yet you obeyed from the heart that form of doctrine to which you were delivered. And having been set free from sin, you became slaves of righteousness.

ROMANS 6:14-18

I speak in human terms because of the weakness of your flesh. For just as you presented your members as slaves of uncleanness, and of lawlessness leading to more lawlessness, so now present your members as slaves of righteousness for holiness. For when you were slaves of sin, you were free in regard to righteousness. What fruit did you have then in the things of which you are now ashamed? For the end of those things is death. But now having been set free from sin, and having become slaves of God, you have your fruit to holiness, and the end, everlasting life. For the wages of sin is death, but the gift of God is eternal life in Christ Jesus our Lord.

ROMANS 6:19-23

This marvelous life God imparts is given so that we might be in service to Him—not to fulfill our own desires and plans. It was not just provided as a way we could escape hell. He wants to deposit Himself into earthen vessels such as you and me.

The Almighty spoke many generations ago that the glory of the Lord would one day fill this earth (Numbers 14:21) and He fully intends to pour that glory through and *out* of us in this awesome finale! Can we comprehend it? Can we fathom such a plan?

We must break away from the sin and darkness of the world and be separated unto Him—to become clean vessels in order to be "this glorious Church" without spot or blemish! Because of Jesus this is possible!

"SIN LUGGAGE"

In these final days we must "reckon ourselves" to be dead to sin; I mean *totally* dead to it! With the power of Almighty God residing inside, we are not to allow sin to rule and reign in our mortal bodies. As His people, we are destined to walk in the same realm as the Lord; we are made in His image!

It should be entirely natural for us to walk with God, yet we can't do it carrying around all this "sin luggage." We've tried sitting on the fence with one foot in the world and the other in the Church, and still we have expected victory. The House of God is filled with saints who are attempting to serve both good and evil. They continue to think and do things that are acceptable to the world—keeping their Christianity low-key in order not to draw attention to themselves. These same people attend church on Sunday *We cannot serve two masters— period!* morning believing they will receive the full blessings of the Lord.

This lifestyle will not work! And when trouble hits them through the doors they've opened because of sinful behavior, they are absolutely astounded!

We cannot serve two masters—period! Jesus said we would hate one and love the other or be loyal to one and despise the other (Matthew 6:24). I suppose we cleave to the one from which we desire the benefits.

131

Since we have been bought with a price; we are no longer our own and are not to present or yield ourselves to sin.

COMING ALIVE!

I believe if we truly understood the cost Jesus paid to redeem us from iniquity—the agony and suffering He experienced and what an astronomical price He paid to set us free—we would not be so nonchalant about sin.

If we knew the love of our Father and truly reciprocated that love, we would tame these mortal bodies. After all, we should no longer have anything in common with the world. All believers understand they should crucify the flesh and the old nature. Unfortunately, even though they know it should be dead, they really don't want it to die!

Sin's behavior doesn't end just because we are born again.

That "dying" part is not something that appeals to us. We know that Jesus gave His life for us, yet if we'd be honest, we would rather not die— even in service to Him. But death is only painful when we don't want to give up what God considers wrong!

We not only have to be dead to sin, but must also "reckon ourselves" to be alive unto God and present ourselves to Him (Romans 6:11). That's the only way we will have the ability and power to remain out of the world system and resist the temptation it offers.

Scripture tells us to overcome evil with good. It takes the enforced Law of the Spirit of Life in Christ Jesus to subdue the law of sin and death (Romans 8:2).

A LIVING SACRIFICE

Sin's *behavior* doesn't end just because we are born again. It takes our cooperation and effort with the Word of

132

God to sever the bad habits of our former lifestyle.

This new life has raised us from the dead so that we can be free from the evil demands of our flesh. Thank God, our carnal man is no longer in control.

It is our fleshly nature that normally gives us the trouble. True, we are still waiting on the redemption of our bodies, when, as Scripture states, mortality is going to put on immortality (1 Corinthians 15:53), but the Word of God within enables each of us to live our days in the power of this new life.

Think about that, Church! By faith we should be walking in the power of our resurrection by the Glory of the Father that resides within us!

We were crucified with Him on the Cross so that our bodies could be loosed from the dead spirits that controlled our actions. We certainly were slaves of sin because we yielded to it continually—that is all our old unregenerate spirits knew. But now, we are to take this life of God that is within us, declare ourselves dead to sin, subdue our body, and present it to God as being alive from the dead. This is truly a living sacrifice, holy and acceptable to Him (Romans 12:1).

In the eyes of God, this is the reality of the new birth.

IN LINE WITH THE WORD

We are to offer our bodies to serve God, making them instruments of righteousness and holy living. Remember, we've been liberated from sin—it no longer has dominion over us! We are to walk free from it by renewing our minds to think in line with the Word, to dominate this flesh so that we can bear righteous and holy fruit for God.

Scripture states we can train this body to know the difference between good and evil *by practice* (Hebrews 5:14 AMP). It can be developed so it flows with our God-indwelt spirit instead of constantly causing us problems.

Seeing ourselves dead to sin as well as alive unto God takes spiritual exercise and practice. And let me say it again: *if we don't talk it, we won't receive it.* We will never rise higher than what our mouth gives us steps to climb, because our words direct the course of our lives.

BENEFITS AND BLESSINGS

No matter which kingdom we serve, there are wages that accompany our service (Romans 6:23). We have a choice: we can continue to be slaves of sin and reap death, or we can serve God and enjoy the results and benefits of eternal life.

In the past, we've yielded to the worldly way of doing things because it was more familiar to us, and also seemed an easier path to travel. The world runs in a negative direction on a broader path, and that's the one most people follow. Yet traveling that road will not produce the godly fruit of eternal life which has already been given to us.

No matter which kingdom we serve, there are wages that accompany our service.

Let me encourage you that as born again Christians, we are not like those who are spiritually dead. Even while we remain in this physical body, we can walk with God every day and serve in total union with Him. The benefits and blessings will be ours!

"THE GREAT I AM"

I trust you are beginning to realize what righteousness has done! When we are conformed to the image of the Lord Jesus and live in union with Him in this glorious life, we travel a higher, more wondrous path.

There is therefore now no condemnation to those who are in Christ Jesus, who do not walk according to the flesh, but according to the Spirit.
ROMANS 8:1

Some read this verse and exclaim, "There's no condemnation in the Lord at all!" They want to believe they won't be condemned regardless of what they do, but that's not what Paul wrote.

This verse declares there is no blame or censure *only* if we are walking after the Spirit and not after our fleshly nature. In fact, 1 John 3 tells us that *our heart* will condemn us if we are not walking in the light of the Word of God.

We can only have confidence with the Father when we are living according to the promptings of our resurrected spirits. The righteousness of God is fulfilled when we walk not after our sinful nature, but after the Spirit.

Too often we forget that we have been bought and paid for—and the One Who paid the price is watching. Most of us don't have a true revelation that we are transporting "The Great I Am" everywhere we go.

TOTAL CONFIDENCE

We must never forget, the Lord sees everything we do. It makes no difference if we close every blind, or paint every window black; there are at least two people who always see what we are doing—ourselves and God. And, if we commit a fleshly act such as to steal or commit adultery, there is condemnation. Our spirit—which is fused to the Holy Spirit—will rise up and convict us.

*And by this we know that we are of the truth,
and shall assure our hearts before Him. For if our
heart condemns us, God is greater than our heart, and
knows all things. Beloved, if our heart does not
condemn us, we have confidence toward God.*

I JOHN 3:19-21

The Holy Spirit is within, teaching us how to be holy and live a righteous life before God and man. Yes, heavenly correction will surface to keep us from continuing down that pathway of sin. I'm even talking about when we eat out in restaurants and sneak home all the extra packets of "Sweet 'n Low" on the table. It's wrong, and our heart knows it!

Walking in righteousness demands that we make adjustments in our lives. For example, if we are to be at work at 8:00 A.M., that doesn't mean we come strolling in at 8:15 because that is stealing time from our employer.

When we give our word we will be at a certain place at a certain time, we need to fulfill our promise and be punctual. In actuality, it may make little difference if we are there or not, but our words will be a lie if we fail to do so.

"LIVE IT," DON'T "TALK IT"

Living out our righteousness means we are people of ethics—living at a higher standard. The true test of our character is not limited to who we are in public, but who we are when we're alone—the person who is in our own heart.

Every day we deal with the temptation to compromise. We're all enticed to walk close to the edge and push the limits. For instance, when we pay a bill and are given too much change, we need to be honest and tell the salesperson. Don't remain quiet and think, "Well, God has blessed me." Instead, we must walk back to the counter and say, "I think you gave me too much money."

If they reply, "Don't worry about it," *then* we are blessed of the Lord.

We must *live* this life, not just talk about it.

THE LIFESTYLE TEST

The reason we can yield righteous fruit is because we are literally dead to sin. It no longer has dominion and we must not allow hell to rule our lives. Satan should not dictate what we do or *don't* do. And since the devil has no authority over us, let's not give him any!

When sin entices us, we can put that temptation on the Cross and consider it dead. By our lifestyle we demonstrate to our family and our employer we are honest and trustworthy—that they can have confidence in us.

> *Since the devil has no authority over us, let's not give him any!*

In Romans 6 we see death and life at the same time; dying to self and living to Him. As we present ourselves to the Lord, He begins to live through us. Instead of saying that "one day" we will be dead to sin, we must see that happening today. God needs us as clean, righteous vessels *here*—to impact our world *now*. And according to the Word, our death to sin has already taken place!

Each time we put off our righteous position until another day, we are giving the devil an extension of control over us. We need to see ourselves as victorious children of the Living God this very moment! In the eyes of the Lord there is no condemnation, inferiority, or guilt—and we are to reign over sin from this heavenly God-ordained position.

What a wondrous life awaits us if we'll just begin the journey. The Lord is here to lift us to a place where the elementary things of this world's system no longer entrap us. By setting our affections on heaven, earth loses its grasp and our freedom in Christ grows.

BREAKING THE DARKNESS

Can we live like this? Can we be the Glorious Church— the remnant that will choose this higher life and walk in fullness and power?

I believe we can. That's why I am admonishing you to join us and become a part of what the Lord is doing. I am convinced that in this great final move of Jehovah, His glory and power will explode and turn the earth upside down once more – just as in the early days of the Church.

When we discover who we are in Christ Jesus, and begin to walk like *somebody* in God, hell will bow its knee. We will be the light that penetrates and breaks the darkness. We'll bring hope to the hopeless and life where death has prevailed.

We'll bring hope to the hopeless and life where death has prevailed.

By knowing *who we know* and *who we are,* it's possible to walk as that resurrected man, full of the Father, the Son, and the Holy Ghost. Then, as we begin to live in righteousness, with humility before God, He will clear the way ahead and hell will not be able to stop the glory that will surely come!

AN OVERCOMER!

Friend, you can only become what God envisions by raising your head and walking uprightly before the Lord—not succumbing to the dictates of your flesh. Living in your past will cause you to miss your future!

We are in no way boasting of ourselves when we talk about righteousness. Instead, we are bragging on the Father, and how by His power, grace, and mercy He is able to live His righteousness out *in* and *through* us. Praise our Wonderful Lord!

> *For whatever is born of God overcomes the world.*
> *And this is the victory that has overcome the world*
> *—our faith. Who is he who overcomes the world, but*
> *he who believes that Jesus is the Son of God?*
> I JOHN 5:4-5

If you have given your heart to Christ you are an overcomer! The Bible says we are "born of God" and thus prevail over the world and its ways.

THE FAITH WALK

Let me ask these questions: Why aren't we seeing more victory in our lives? When God says we absolutely overcome every situation and circumstance of life because we are born of Him, why are we not seeing that total victory?

I believe it is because we are not acting on what is said in the above verse—we are not operating in faith. Instead, we are being swayed by what we see or feel, not what the Word of God has declared.

Every victory we ever experience is because we walk not by sight, but by faith. In the midst of the hellish things swirling around us we must stand immovable, confessing what God said about the situation. When we believe that we are overcomers, well, *we overcome!* The one who conquers knows that Jesus is the Son of God.

The Bible is clear that from heaven's point of view, we are righteous, and have certain rights and privileges that come with our inheritance as a child of God.

When we confess the devil has us on the run and it looks like he is winning, we are in error. Sure, we've all felt that way—that we were being ambushed and fading fast. However, what we were actually saying is, at that moment, we were not sensing our righteousness. We were being moved by what we *felt*: "God is not listening to my prayers. Nothing is happening. He's nowhere around!"

That is the time to stop and declare: "But the prayers of the righteous man avail much and I am righteous in Him!" Address the situation through the Word and the victory of the Cross. We have *already* conquerored! The devil is under our feet!

BY THE BOOK!

Here's the problem. We have not yet made ourselves victors in our own heart. My friend, we cannot triumph if we don't know with surety we are already conquerors according to Scripture. The Word of God is the truth, regardless of what we might feel or think about the situation.

The reason we can know and believe we have overcome is because it is written in the Book! Talk to yourself and meditate on the Scriptures until they are fully planted in your heart. We must be convinced that "Greater is He Who is in me than he who is in the world!"

With the confidence of the Creator, we know there is no circumstance of life that God cannot remedy! Too often, we remain earthly minded, centered on the problem rather than the solution. We even ignore the power of God's Word that can deliver us.

Do you see why we must make a diligent effort to keep moving toward God—to keep thinking His thoughts and speaking His Word? Unless we persevere, the law of sin and death will continue to drive us, even though we have been redeemed.

"JUST DO IT!"

In order to be vessels of honor fit for the Master's use, we must no longer keep lying in bed with the world. Since we have been made into the righteousness of God in Christ Jesus, we must live in that privilege and walk as the Spirit-indwelt saints we are!

Righteousness and power go hand in hand. Believing what we are in Christ will automatically change how we live. We walk "right" before God and man because we honor the death, burial, and resurrection of our Savior. The Lord is searching for someone who will stand up and "just do it" based on what He proclaims, not on what we feel.

Righteousness and power go hand in hand.

All of heaven knows and understands the position born again saints have in the Kingdom of God—but all of hell knows it too. So the devil's strategy is to keep us ignorant and deceived, detoured from walking in the paths of truth. Satan doesn't want us to act on what we certainly have the power and authority to accomplish. Let me remind you the devil is the father of lies. Satan is hoping we won't see the depths of the Blood of Jesus and what it did—and continues to do—for us! The devil is doing everything in his power to keep us from taking the step of faith that moves us boldly into our righteous position.

In a world filled with darkness and evil, we have the God-given ability to be separated from it.

LIKE FLASHLIGHTS

The older I become, and the more I walk with God, the

stronger I recognize the power of our tongue to put into motion what we believe.

Every day, we need to consistently affirm and declare what God's Word says concerning us. Our words resemble flashlights, dividing the darkness before us as we walk— shining the light we need to live in holiness and righteousness.

What we say can activate the switch of our faith to the "on" position and illuminate the valley of death! It can clear the pathway for us to travel unharmed. Truly, our mouth can show us the traps of hell as we proclaim the oracles of the Almighty.

Child of God, stop speaking about the negative side of life. Oh, we might throw out some righteous-sounding sentences, but when we get down to the nitty-gritty, we start talking the problem again. When that happens, we turn off the light and return to the world's system of darkness where hell can ensnare us.

WILL YOU YIELD?

It grieves my heart the Church has forgotten that our God is Holy and we are to be like Him. Yet, there are those who refuse to yield to authority and balk at pastors who establish biblical standards of behavior for their flock. Many Christians would rather have a "modern" God—Who will tolerate their laziness and sinful actions. My friend, Jehovah won't do that! He sets marks of spiritual excellence for us to reach and invites us to that high calling.

It is impossible to experience a *real* encounter with God and have everything remain as it was before that time. You see, when the Father does something for us, it demands our action. So, if we've been attending church for years yet nothing in our home has changed—if our former routine has not been disturbed—something is missing. We need to fall on our faces before God in true repentance.

Everything the Lord has for us comes out of His glory—out of His character. Righteousness propels us into that glorious realm. And the more we live under what He has provided, the more we move toward His glory.

There are those who may say "In the Name of Jesus" to everything they do, yet it is very obvious nothing ever changes for them. That happens when people have a religious understanding, but have not yet moved into the reality of fellowship with God—where the Lord is real and evident in their lives.

What will it take for the Church – and for you personally – to radiate the glory of the Father to the world? That day will come when we totally yield ourselves to righteousness.

CHAPTER 9

THE BLOOD, THE CROSS, AND THE EXCHANGE

Sometime, somewhere, somehow, the dilemma of the Original Sin had to be solved.

We know that when Adam and Eve were in the Garden of Eden they sinned by disobeying God and turning away from their Creator. Here's what we often overlook. Certainly, Eve was deceived by the serpent, but Scripture reveals that Adam was not fooled (1 Timothy 2:14). He knew exactly what was taking place.

Adam was standing beside his wife when the serpent was speaking to her (Genesis 3:6). He was well aware they were disobeying God's instructions and turning their back on Him.

From the moment they ate of the forbidden fruit, dramatic changes immediately occurred. Satan now ruled mankind and with his reign came his evil "signature" of sin and death that held every man in captivity throughout generations.

Although man was created in the image and splendor of Almighty God, in that dreadful moment, we fell into spiritual poverty, alienated from the life and presence of

Jehovah. We no longer looked like the Creator on the inside. Instead, we had fallen from grandeur into darkness. After that initial sin, man could not pay the price to make things right with God—there was a debt on us that we would *never* be able to repay.

BREAKING THE CHAINS

Thank God for the plan that was established from before the foundation of the world. It was designed to redeem man back to our original glorious state, free from the chains of death that held us in bondage!

When mankind chose to walk away from God and leave Him out of their lives, there was not one single thing in the universe that demanded the Father had to deal with man ever again—*except* His love for us! And that is what Calvary is all about!

The life of the Father that was in His Blood broke the power of sin that dominated us.

It took God Himself—not just an innocent man, but Deity—to come and shed His Blood, to pay the debt that held us in the slavery of death. Scripture states that without the shedding of blood there is no remission of sin —and what flowed from Christ on Calvary more than qualified. The life of the Father that was in His Blood broke the power of sin that dominated us.

So the Word came and indwelt a body of flesh that was prepared for Him. And Jesus, the Son of God, walked on this earth the way the Creator intended for the *first* Adam to walk. Jesus lived uprightly before God and man—a totally sinless life, never in opposition or disobedience to His Father.

145

OUR SUBSTITUTE

At the appointed time, Jesus died for us; the Godly for the ungodly, the Innocent for the guilty. On that Cross He was our Substitute. Most important, there were divine exchanges that took place—exchanges that brought us great victory!

Jesus became like us so we could become like Him! He hung on that Cross and shed His Blood for all mankind to redeem and reconcile us back to God. He then descended into the pit of hell—because that is where man was destined to go without redemption. Man, without God or His Son, will split the gates of hell wide open.

Three days and three nights were spent by our Lord in the bowels of the earth. But, thanks be to God, He was raised by the power of the Spirit! He returned victorious with the keys of death, hell, and the grave in His possession (Revelation 1:18). He is the Champion of our Salvation—for all men, for all times!

BLOOD-BOUGHT!

Jesus, the first to be born from the dead, presented Himself before God, and took His precious life-giving Blood behind the veil into the Heavenly Holy of Holies. He poured that Blood on the Mercy Seat made for you and me, to enable us to walk in freedom in every area of our lives.

Triumph over Satan was completed on the Cross (Galatians 1:4), yet we cannot claim the victory of Calvary without first understanding the miraculous work of the Blood of the Lamb. We cannot participate in *any* of our benefits of righteousness without first having passed through the precious Blood of our Lord Jesus.

I think most Christians have missed the power in the Cross itself. That's where the Blood brought the necessary exchanges and Satan was defeated—and it was the Cross that enabled this to occur. We really can't separate these things, yet each produced a distinct power that is available to us for different areas of our lives.

THE COMPLETED WORK

If we could only see ourselves through the precious Blood of our Savior, and know in reality that His life was literally poured out for us, we would choose to live a crucified life. You see, when we refer to the Blood of Jesus, we are always talking about dealing with sin. Calvary's Cross speaks of our Messiah hanging there as our Substitute—the Righteous dying for the unrighteous. Of course, we can't have the power of the Cross released without the Blood which flowed.

However, what happened at Calvary gives us another dimension—the full redemption, or what some people call the *completed* work of the Cross.

Please understand, we are in no way downplaying the power of the Blood! We thank God for it—that's what ransomed and cleansed us from sin so we could come into the presence of The Father. It wiped out all the filth of yesterday so we can walk in the wonderful benefits of the Cross. Yet, the Blood of the Lord by itself does not heal our bodies. And if

We claim our healing on the fullness of what happened at Calvary.

we don't understand the Blood—and what it purchased for us—we will not enter the healing process at all because our past will control us. We claim our healing on the fullness of what happened on Calvary.

DEALING WITH PAST MISTAKES

We need to place everything that happened at Calvary in

perspective. You and I have been made righteous because of what the Blood accomplished on the Cross. It enables us to leave our yesterdays and move into the bright future of tomorrow. Satan knows that we—as children of the Living God—are righteous in the eyes of the Almighty. As such, he fully understands we are more powerful than he! Yet, the devil doesn't want *us* to know that!

It's true the Blood of Jesus redeemed us, but if we do not stay centered on the power of the Blood and what it completed on that rugged Cross, we will continue living in "sin consciousness." In such a state, every time we try to move forward spiritually, the devil will bring us back to "who we used to be" and "what we used to do." As a result we will be defeated—even though by the truth of Almighty God we are surely overcomers of the world, the flesh, and the devil.

The Blood washed away all the filth of unrighteousness and it has not lost any of its power!

If our past mistakes continually harass us and cause us to back off from the benefits of eternal life, we have not accepted the full effectiveness of the Blood. We must stand in the fact that at Calvary, the Blood washed away all the filth of unrighteousness and it has not lost any of its power!

THE BENEFITS

Experiencing full victory in this life requires that we walk in the work of the Blood *as well as the benefits of the Cross.* Many saints know their sins are forgiven, but have little victory in their lives. If we don't understand what God purchased for us on Calvary, we simply will be happy saying, "My sins are buried and I'm heaven bound"—yet we face defeat continually while living out our days here on earth.

My friend, if we are held back by such thinking, we will not be the message of hope to others that He has destined us to be. Thank God our sins are forgiven, and I praise Him that He accomplished these specific exchanges for us. Because of the sacrifice of Jesus on the Cross of Calvary, there are certain things we just don't have to tolerate!

What gives many believers monumental trouble is the fact that the power of the Blood does not deal totally with our fleshly nature. We can plead the Blood of Jesus over our flesh till the cows come home, and it will do nothing to alleviate our bad habits and worldly behavior.

Please understand, it is impossible to educate the flesh to do what is right. Oh, we may try to reform our carnal nature to God's standards by going to self-help groups or by applying pressure to stop behaving in a certain way. We attempt to reprogram ourselves so that we are "in control" of our actions. As a result, we make resolutions that last about two weeks.

What does the Bible tell us to do with our fleshly nature? We are to *crucify it* and to mortify its deeds.

A COVER UP?

Calvary talks about dying while the Blood speaks of cleansing and redeeming. Satan camouflages our good efforts for a short time to make us think we are winning. Then, at some unsuspected moment, our old nature will resurface. Why? Because instead of crucifying it, we only painted it over and pretended it wasn't there—thinking it was conquered!

Unfortunately, we never understood that our flesh was dead, even though we were crucified with Jesus the moment of our new birth. If something is dead, we shouldn't allow it to have one more breath of life!

DR. SANDRA G. KENNEDY

"I am going to do better," we say. "I'm not going to take that drink"—and other proclamations of our carnal nature. What we are actually saying is "Flesh, I can control you"— yet the flesh will make a liar of us every time!

Churches are filled with people who know nothing of a crucified life, and refuse to talk about the Blood! There will never be victory for those living under such deception. It's time for God's people to stand on what the Bible says and let the old nature die.

STARTING OVER

I'm glad to announce the Lord can give you a brand new life—so that you can start all over again. From the Father's point of view, He is not dealing with the *old man*; He dealt with it on Calvary once and for all. According to the Word, we were crucified with Him on the Cross.

If we are going to have an intimate relationship with the Lord, and walk in our righteousness, we must see ourselves dead to iniquity and any unrighteous behavior. Think of it! We are dead to sin because of the Blood of Jesus and alive to God because the old man has passed away!

J have been crucified with Christ; it is no longer
J who live, but Christ lives in me; and the life which
J now live in the flesh J live by faith in the Son
of God, who loved me and gave Himself for me.
GALATIANS 2:20

We've tried to apply the Blood to change our behavior and make it cleanse the flesh, and it does not. That is one reason many are not walking in victory. Let me say it this way: we are basically pleading the Blood at the wrong moments. We should be claiming the full victory of Calvary, yet once again, we can't do that unless we know what was accomplished there. We must be knowledgeable of the benefits of the new birth and the inheritance which belongs to the sons and daughters of God.

> *Inasmuch then as the children have partaken*
> *of flesh and blood, He Himself likewise shared*
> *in the same, that through death He might destroy*
> *him who had the power of death, that is, the devil,*
> *and release those who through fear of death were*
> *all their lifetime subject to bondage.*
> HEBREWS 2:14-15

What destroyed the devil and his kingdom and released us from bondage? Jesus' death on the Cross of Calvary! And in order for us to walk in full victory, we must learn to claim not only the power of that precious Blood (which always refers to sin), but also learn to declare the triumph of Calvary over our enemy, the devil!

> *And they overcame him by the blood of the*
> *Lamb and by the word of their testimony, and*
> *they did not love their lives to the death.*
> REVELATION 12:11

When Satan's accusations pertain to sin, we can overcome those charges by the Blood of the Lamb—because the Blood deals with sin. The verse above goes even further. It tells us the overcomer uses *testimony*, not only of the Blood, but our pronouncement that we do not love our lives unto death. In other words, we live and act in the spirit of the Cross! Crucified! We are no longer ruled by the dictates of our flesh, but are dead to those things—and we allow God to live in and through us in newness of life.

There it is: overcomers are those who know and speak of

the power of the Blood, and also of the power of the Cross and the crucified life.

> *And those who are Christ's have crucified the flesh with its passions and desires. If we live in the Spirit, let us also walk in the Spirit.*
>
> GALATIANS 5:24-25

Those of us who have accepted Jesus as our Lord and Savior—and walk as such—have seen what Calvary accomplished and understand the principles of Romans 6. When we begin to live out our righteousness in Christ Jesus we have taken hold of the truth that our old man has, indeed, been crucified—that it is no longer us who lives but Christ Jesus living in us.

THE CLEANSINIG

Most churches ignore the fact that the only way God deals with His people is on the grounds we've been crucified. He works with us through the Blood of Jesus, but also through the power of the Cross. In fact, the only flesh the Blood protects is flesh that has gone to Calvary to mortify its deeds.

The Bible tells us the Blood of Jesus continually cleanses only those believers who walk in the light as God is in the Light. You see, when the Father looks at us, He sees us through the Blood of the Lord hanging on Calvary. God sees us dead to sin, free from our old nature, and cleansed by the Blood of the Lamb. And we are required to live this in daily practice in order to have full victory.

Sadly, many are busy acting like they are the same people, only with new clothes on, "dolled up," or just adopting a new vocabulary for church. That's not what the Lord desires.

We are *new people,* living in our old bodies with its bad

habits—and it takes the Word of the Living God to make that situation work to the point it is pleasing to Him! We have to mortify the deeds of our flesh using the Word so that this new man (our new spirit), created in righteousness and true holiness, is able to express itself without interference.

COMING TOGETHER

For the Church to flow as one body, we *all* must do this. Those within the Body of Christ who like their old nature and prefer themselves just as they are, cannot in any way have unity with those of us who recognize that we are new creatures in Christ Jesus.

Righteousness and unrighteousness are not compatible. Truly, this is one of the major reasons there are so many splits within the Church—so many factions, so much confusion. The dead thing and the new thing will never be in harmony, even though there have been so many attempts to reconcile them as one. People assume that because we all wear the label of "Christian" we have the same content in our hearts; but not so.

People assume that because we all wear the label of "Christian" we have the same content in our hearts; but not so.

THE GREAT RECONCILIATION

Let's take a closer look at the amazing exchanges that took place while Jesus hung on the Cross. They were ordained by God, Himself—all part of the great reconciliation and restoration He had in His heart from the beginning.

We truly have been reconciled with God and there is absolutely no wedge that stands between us or alienates us from our Holy Father. Our failure has been nailed to the Cross! True reconciliation, indeed, has been accomplished for us through our Savior, Jesus Christ!

There is absolutely no wedge that stands between us or alienates us from our Holy Father.

The books of Leviticus and Hebrews tell us that there is no remission of sin without the shedding of blood because *life* is in the blood. From the red liquid of a tiny animal to the Blood of Jesus Himself, the life is carried within the contents of their blood.

THE BLOOD COVERS ALL!

The Bible records four separate places where Jesus shed His Blood in His last hours on earth. The first was in the Garden of Gethsemane as He prayed to the Father before He went to the Cross. In agony, His heart began to burst and *"...his sweat was as it were great drops of blood falling down to the ground"* (Luke 22:44 KJV).

The second location was when Jesus was in the hall of Pilate. It was there He was whipped and scourged without mercy. In the book of Leviticus we read where the children of Israel were instructed to skin and rip open the animal sacrifice. Jesus fulfilled what was written in the law. His flesh was ripped as He was beaten with a Roman "cat of nine tails"—a whip with pieces of metal embedded that tear into the body.

The third time His Blood spilled during this horrendous ordeal was when the crown of thorns was placed on His head —forced on His brow and beaten into His skull. Again the life of God was poured out and His Blood touches every part of us. You see, Calvary addressed the spiritual issue, but His Blood took care of the physical issue. Jesus came teaching repentance and healing, meeting both of those needs.

Finally, in the fourth area, the soldiers pierced His hands, His feet, and His side—and the Blood freely flowed.

There is not one inch of us, from the top of our head to the bottom of our feet, that is not covered by His Blood or unaffected by the Cross! What a God we serve!

> *Who has believed our report? And to whom has the arm of the Lord been revealed? For He shall grow up before Him as a tender plant, And as a root out of dry ground. He has no form or comeliness; And when we see Him, There is no beauty that we should desire Him. He is despised and rejected by men, A man of sorrows and acquainted with grief. And we hid, as it were, our faces from Him; He was despised, and we did not esteem Him. Surely He has borne our griefs and carried our sorrows; Yet we esteemed Him stricken, Smitten by God, and afflicted. But He was wounded for our transgressions, He was bruised for our iniquities; The chastisement for our peace was upon Him, And by His stripes we are healed.*
>
> ISAIAH 53:1-5

Look at that question again: "Who has believed our report?"

The answer I would give is that very *few* believe—even within the Church of the Living God! The Body of Christ, infused with the Spirit of the Lord, empowered by the Word, set free by the Blood of the Lamb has not, for the most part, seen this great Divine Exchange.

THE PROMISE FULFILLED

The prophet Isaiah had great insight into the death of the coming Messiah on the Cross – which would occur hundreds of years later. He actually "saw" more than those who eventually stood at Calvary and watched the scene unfold first hand. Even the disciples did not understand what was taking place in front of their eyes.

The Cross defeated Satan completely and forever! In the eyes of God, the devil is not only under *His* feet, but under ours as well!

Biblical faith is simply a recognition of the truths declared in the Word of God and the integrity of our Heavenly Father. It's easy to walk in faith when we can see a full view of the Cross and what was done for us there. It's a matter of believing He fulfilled what He promised.

SEVEN EXCHANGES

What took place at Calvary was far more than one exchange; there were *seven*. Let me share them with you:

Exchange Number One: Punishment for peace.

When Jesus hung on the Cross and said, "It is finished," those words were so much more than the fulfillment of the law. He took the punishment we deserved to give us peace with God—to bring complete wholeness.

Exchange number two: Unrighteousness for righteousness.

At Calvary, Jesus bore our sins and failures and gave us His right-standing with God. He went to hell on our behalf— the Just for the unjust—so that we might come into the presence of Almighty God once again.

Exchange number three: The curse for the blessing.

As our Savior hung on the Cross, He bore the curse for breaking the law so the blessings that were promised to Abraham might come on the Gentiles by faith in Christ Jesus. We read of these blessings of obedience and the curses of disobedience in Deuteronomy 28. He became the curse for us so that we need not bear them if we are walking with God!

Exchange number four: Sickness for health.

By the stripes that were inflicted on His back in Pilate's court, we are healed (1 Peter 2:24), and while hanging on that Cross, He took within Him every sickness and every pain that we might go free!

Exchange number five: Poverty for prosperity.

Poverty in any form – including hunger, thirst, nakedness and lack" is under the curse of the law. He endured it and broke its power just for you and me! We know that by His grace, *"...though He was rich, yet for your sakes He became poor, that you through His poverty might become rich"* (2 Corinthians 8:9). The state of being rich does not just include finances, although money is certainly part of it; but it is a grace given by God to us more fully explained in the following verse: *"And God is able to make all grace abound toward you, that you, always having all sufficiency in all things, may have an abundance for every good work"* (2 Corinthians 9:8).

Exchange number six: Rejection for acceptance.

Jesus was separated from God just as we were, yet He became like us so that we could become like Him—one with God! He took our rejection and gave us His acceptance before the Father and there is now nothing that stands between us. We are His workmanship created in Christ Jesus unto good works.

Exchange number seven: Death for life.

At the Cross, He died as our Substitute so we might walk in the newness of His eternal life forever and ever! Death no longer has any sting for us! We have the promise of heaven as our home: where He is we may be also.

SO MUCH MORE!

My friend, ignorance and unbelief are the two barriers that cause us to miss everything that God has provided. They are the reasons we do not walk in victory.

Let me ask again: "Who *has* believed the report of the Lord?"

Carnal Christians are really those who do not understand the benefits of Calvary—and the divine exchanges that took place there. Yes, the Blood was poured out for your iniquity, yet Jesus bore the penalty of sin that we might have so much more!

With every fiber that is within me, I am asking you to make the decision to receive what took place at the Cross. May the old become new, and death become life!

CHAPTER 10

THE ROBE: FROM NOAH TO NOW!

Who was the first person on earth to be called "righteous"? It was Noah. Yet, even before his time, events were taking place that forced man to choose good or evil, right or wrong, righteousness or wickedness.

Let's take a closer look at what happened within the Garden of Eden. How wondrous it must have been to reside in that beautiful place! All things God could possibly offer to mankind were there at his disposal. The Lord Himself walked with Adam and Eve in the cool of the day and He blessed them beyond measure. It was their Father's good pleasure to give them the Kingdom!

Then God blessed them, and God said to them,
"Be fruitful and multiply; fill the earth and subdue it; have dominion over the fish of the sea, over the birds of the air, and over every living thing that moves on the earth."
GENESIS 1:28

Mankind was empowered by the Lord to rule and reign as

kings on this planet. Everything was perfect; there was no evil of any kind. It must have been a glorious place.

Then God saw everything that He
had made, and indeed it was very good...
GENESIS 1:31

The desire of the Creator was to protect mankind so that His goodness could flow to them all the days of their lives. He announced only one "do not"—an instruction given to provide and insure life. Had the first man and woman adhered to God's warning, the world would have been so different.

And the Lord God commanded the man, saying,
"Of every tree of the garden you may freely eat; but of the
tree of the knowledge of good and evil you shall not eat, for
in the day that you eat of it you shall surely die."
GENESIS 2:16-17

God so loved mankind that He didn't want His creation to even know about wickedness, much less deal with it continually. That's why He asked Adam and Eve not to eat of the tree of knowledge of good and evil.

However, because of their disobedience, iniquity began to run rampant without restraint. And according to the words God spoke that day, the first man and woman surely died. Oh, they did not physically, since they lived another 900-plus years, but they died spiritually—they were separated from the life of God.

Before eternal damage would be done, however, Adam and Eve were ousted from the Garden.

THE PLAN!

The tree of life is important. There seems to be no limitation given by God to restrain them from continuing to eat of this forbidden fruit. Had they eaten of the tree of life in their *fallen* condition, however, there would have been no hope for man throughout eternity—their fate would have been sealed in doom. So in the grace and mercy of God, He removed them from the Garden and stationed an angel to guard its gate.

Yet, according to God's fore-knowledge of this event, there was a plan established and already in operation. The Scripture is clear: The Lamb of God—the Redeemer—had been slain from before the foundation of the world. In truth, the Redeeming Blood had already been shed before God ever created man. Mankind was not forever lost from His Creator! The design was in place to redeem us back to God and restore us to our original glory.

> *In truth, the Redeeming Blood had already been shed before God ever created man.*

THE PROMISED LINEAGE

You remember that two curses were pronounced as a result of the fall; one upon the earth (ground) and one upon Satan. Neither man nor woman was cursed.

Of course, there were results and consequences of their disobedience such as suffering with childbirth and working by the sweat of their brow, but there was no curse pronounced upon mankind at that time. Even though this has been taught for years, it is simply not what the Bible states.

This couple initially bore two sons, Cain and Abel. Out of anger, Cain rose up against his brother and murdered him.

Then another son, Seth, was born to Adam and his wife along with other children. Seth was the one chosen through whom the promised lineage would come that would bring forth the Messiah, the Savior of the world. However, Seth was not made in the initial splendor of his father, Adam.

This is the book of the genealogy of Adam.
In the day that God created man, He made him
in the likeness of God. And Adam lived one hundred
and thirty years, and begot a son in his own likeness,
after his image, and named him Seth.
GENESIS 5:1,3

Notice the Scripture tells us Seth was born in Adam's image—not in the image of Almighty God. The death seed within Adam was being passed down to all his children, even though Seth would be in the divine lineage of Jesus. However, after a son was born to Seth, something interesting happens. Men once again begin to call on the Name of the Lord.

And as for Seth, to him also a son was
born; and he named him Enosh. Then men
began to call on the name of the Lord.
GENESIS 4:26

A few generations after Enosh, a man named Enoch was born. He is the first individual recorded in Scripture who actually preached. He proclaimed the message of God to the people of his day, telling them in everyday language, that if they didn't straighten up, they would suffer—because there is a penalty for sin.

By faith, Enoch was "raptured" away and never faced

death because of his testimony and the fact he walked with God (Hebrews 11:5; Genesis 5:24).

> *Now Enoch, the seventh from Adam, prophesied*
> *about these men also, saying, "Behold, the Lord comes*
> *with ten thousands of His saints, to execute judgment*
> *on all, to convict all who are ungodly among them of all*
> *their ungodly deeds which they have committed in an*
> *ungodly way, and of all the harsh things which*
> *ungodly sinners have spoken against Him."*
> JUDE 14-15

Enoch was the great grandfather of Noah—whom the Bible calls "a righteous man." Yet, the world in which he lived was filled with depravity. Men had become so wicked that the heart of God was grieved at His creation.

> *Then the Lord saw that the wickedness of man*
> *was great in the earth, and that every intent of the*
> *thoughts of his heart was only evil continually. And the*
> *Lord was sorry that He had made man on the earth, and He was*
> *grieved in His heart. So the Lord said, "I will destroy man whom I*
> *have created from the face of the earth, both man and beast, creeping*
> *thing and birds of the air, for I am sorry that I have made them."*
> *But Noah found grace in the eyes of the Lord. This is the genealogy*
> *of Noah. Noah was a just man, perfect in his*
> *generations. Noah walked with God.*
> GENESIS 6:5-9

As we have shared in previous chapters, righteousness is the ability to stand in the presence of God without condemnation, inferiority, or guilt.

When I read the above verses I was fascinated by the fact

that Noah was a just man, perfect in his generations. I kept asking myself, "How could Noah be called righteous at this particular time when the world was already declared in such corruption that the Creator was sorry He made man?" I wondered, "What guided God's grace on Noah? What did this man do in righteousness that enabled him and his family to be saved from the coming wrath?"

How in the world did this ever happen to me?"

These questions are relevant today. Now, as then, corruption is rampant and the evil intentions of man's heart are brazen and without conscience. Media portrays immorality in print and on film that would have stunned us only ten years ago. It seems *anything* goes! It is horrific to witness the depravity of what most people call "humor" and "entertainment." And if we are not careful—not watchful—we will become accustomed to it. Before we know what has happened we become desensitized to sin and it begins to appear in *our* house.

"HOW DID I GET HERE?"

Satan is deceptive. He fails to remind us that we *will* reap a harvest from *every* seed we allow him to plant in our heart! He may start by feeding us only a small amount, yet even that is harmful. Eventually it becomes "every day stuff" and the cutting edge of the sin is removed. Suddenly, we no longer find ourselves willing to fight; so we accept the evil in varying degrees. Then, before we recognize what has taken place, we are in over our heads and wonder, "How in the world did this ever happen to me? How did I get here?"

I'll tell you how! It is the same way people pack on too many pounds—they keep eating one more piece of cake, munching on another slice, until they've eaten the whole thing! I'm sure you understand.

"LET ME IN!"

The fact that Noah was "just and righteous" in the eyes of God is what separated this man from all others on earth. And we are not talking about only a handful of people, but multiplied thousands, perhaps *millions*, because over 1600 years had passed since the creation of man.

Picture the scene. While Noah and his family were lifted above the circumstances of disaster, we forget that there were countless drownings in the great flood that came upon the earth. The Bible doesn't record it, but most likely there were multitudes screaming and clawing on the ark, shouting "Let me in! Let me in!"

We just draw a cute picture for our children of an ark with little animals going aboard and forget the horrendous sight that was occurring because of the depravity of man!

I am reminding you of this because of events today. If something doesn't change soon, surely we will face a similar devastation.

TIME TO WAKE UP!

The only hope for our nation—and for this world—is for the Body of Christ to demonstrate who we are in Christ Jesus. We must stand together, united against this darkness, and pray that God will open hearts to hear the message of the Cross.

We have a responsibility. If we think we can only be concerned about "our four and no more" we are highly deceived! Now is the time for men and women of righteousness to stand tall and proclaim the Word of the Lord. God is counting on you and me!

Church, we are not only talking about our future, but those of men and women who do not yet know the Lord! The value of the Body of Christ to this dying society is wrapped up in the word "righteousness"—and what we do with what we have been given!

As believers, we cannot continue to float on beds of ease, as if the stench of this world does not affect us personally. It's time to wake up! To this point, our protection has been the guarding hand of the Lord. But I sincerely believe if we do not stay locked in, prayed up and speaking words of righteousness, the Lord will remove His shield from us.

God is counting on you and me!

You see, God will only go so far—He must have our cooperation to work and change things. Certainly, He has the power to perform whatever He wishes, yet has designed another plan. Instead, He has chosen to use His Church to accomplish His will on the earth. That's why He desperately needs us to take His Word and defeat the enemy – to rise up and be the Church Victorious!

IT'S NOT AUTOMATIC

Just because we are stamped "righteous" doesn't mean we automatically act that way. Each of us must claim what has been declared in the Word—to take our inheritance and rise above situations and circumstances. Only those who believe, trust, and live it out by faith will become the remnant God uses.

It is not the person who is just *proclaimed* to be righteous by God Almighty that moves into victory, but one who will act out by faith what He has already declared over us.

I hope you understand that the Lord wants the next

"boat" to be filled with His people, but it takes a righteous person to board – a man or woman who, by faith, lives out what God has given him—someone who has been through the sanctification process and demonstrates an "acquitted" life before God and man.

OUR ESCAPE

The account of Noah is so much more than a children's Bible story—although that's what we have made it. It explains how living a righteous life has great benefits and rewards. It shows us we can surely escape the corruption of this world and the devastation to come.

God's plan is not designed only for *our* escape, but that we become a life preserver for others—now and until the day His Son returns. Our actions, attitudes, and words dictate to a great degree whether or not the will of the Lord is accomplished on this earth.

For Christ also suffered once for sins, the just
for the unjust, that He might bring us to God,
being put to death in the flesh but made alive by
the Spirit, by whom also He went and preached to the
spirits in prison, who formerly were disobedient, when
once the Divine longsuffering waited in the days of
Noah, while the ark was being prepared, in which
a few, that is, eight souls, were saved through water.
1 PETER 3:18-20

...and did not spare the ancient world, but saved Noah,
one of eight people, a preacher of righteousness, bringing in
the flood on the world of the ungodly [italics mine]....
2 PETER 2:5

Scripture doesn't record whether his family believed his message, but they were obviously saved by the grace and goodness of God shown toward Noah.

In the midst of the depravity of his civilization, Noah preached righteousness. He not only proclaimed it, he *lived* it! Yet, no one listened. They paid attention only to what he was building and labeled him a fool because they did not understand in the natural what he was doing. However, the Lord waited and withheld judgment while the ark was being prepared by this righteous man.

THE FINAL COUNTDOWN

It is the same in this hour. Our ark should be well under construction by now in the spirit realm as we live out a righteous, sanctified life before others. We are the "Bible" the world is reading and it's time we portrayed an accurate picture of God! He will withhold judgment as long as possible while our ark is being made ready, but He can't wait forever.

Our ark should be well under construction.

I am urging you to prepare and present yourself as a holy vessel unto God.

Perhaps you are reading this book and still insist on looking at how things appear in the natural, refusing to "hear" with your spiritual ears. Don't call these words foolish. My friend, the final countdown has begun and we desperately need to move with God!

FOREWARNED!

In every major event recorded in Scripture, the people were forewarned. Yet again and again, those who should have been prepared were not. Noah tried to explain to everyone what he was building, and what was about to take place, yet no one listened. You would have thought at least one person would have caught on and said, "I repent," but they didn't.

In the midst of the mocking crowds, Noah just kept preaching. Then one day it started to rain. This was something new—and it didn't seem harmful at first. But the clouds grew darker and the rain kept falling until the earth was saturated. Then the waters began to rise!

When God is about to act, He forewarns, yet the precise moment of His arrival is never clear. We know *something* is coming and as long as we are paying attention to the move of His Spirit there is time for preparation.

The Lord waits as long as He can while we are preparing our ark of protection—then suddenly it begins.

The birth of the Savior was prophesied over and over, yet it was missed by the multitudes. The baby born in Bethlehem was not the only child who came into the world that day. The difference was that instructions and details had been given through the centuries concerning this *particular* baby.

Throughout Scripture it was stated that a child would be born under certain circumstances in a certain place. And Jesus came to earth.

Later, as He grew to be a Man and preached to the multitudes, there came another Word from the Lord: "I am going to the Cross"—and He told what would occur (Luke 13:35; 19:43,44; 21:20-24). Yet no one understood.

READY? WATCHING?

Jesus spoke of the fact that He would die, but in three days He would come up out of the grave. The only ones to believe were the enemies of God. Not one disciple showed up at the tomb, awaiting the great event that was about to unfold that Sunday morning. Who was there? Only the guards of the Roman government took Jesus at His word.

On that resurrection day, women stopped by to finish putting spices on His body in the tomb, but no one really believed or understood that He was going to rise from the dead, or they would have been there—ready, watching, anticipating His appearance. Their hearing and comprehension must have been dull since Jesus had told them several times what would occur.

How could it be that those who loved Him so much missed what He said? Why did people who didn't even know Him listen?

What about you and me? Is our hearing any better? Have we heard the Gospel so much that we've lost the reality of its truth? The rapture *is* on the horizon. We may not know the day or the hour, but He *is* coming for those who are ready. Judgment *is* ahead—and so is tribulation.

Have we prepared our ark? Are we living a Godly life before the witnesses of heaven and earth? Have we truly endeavored to plant the Word in our heart as a Shield and a Buckler? Or have we forgotten that the Word is God and failed to honor and esteem it as such?

Awake to righteousness, and do not sin...
I CORINTHIANS 15:34

GOD'S FINEST HOUR

What a grand time lies just ahead for those who are prepared to move into it! Victory is in our heritage! The power of God will fill this earth and flood the nations with glory mankind has yet to behold! Can our Precious Lord count on us to be there for Him—to hold out the rod as Moses did, or stay the sun as Joshua? Do we live as clean vessels before Him in thanksgiving for the mercy and grace

He has shown to us?

He willingly gave Himself because He loved us. Should we do any less for Him?

This will be God's finest hour as He sweeps through the nations by the Spirit of Grace, filling His house with sons and daughters. And we can be a part of it! How glorious it will be – to be used of the Father in such intensity!

Friend, stop and listen to the Shepherd of your Soul. Hear His voice and pay attention to His heart's cry. Listen as He speaks.

Will the days ahead be glory for all of God's children? To be truthful, no. Not all of His sons and daughters are walking uprightly or are prepared for these coming days. Only living in our righteousness will prepare us for what lies ahead.

Noah and his family were saved from—and rose above— the wrath of God. They were not partakers of the destruction that completely surrounded them. Please notice though, they were not transferred to another world while the devastation happened on this one. Righteousness elevated them to ride above it!

PUT ON YOUR ROBE!

Now is the time, my friend, to awaken to our right-standing with the Great Judge of All, and sin not. When we truly come alive to the wondrous, almost incomprehensible gift of righteousness:

- We will give up iniquity, because sin will lose its power over us.
- We will know not only the great benefits of our right-standing with Him, but will understand the grand honor He has given us to be His representatives in this earth.

- We will set our attention and desires on the things of heaven.
- Our hearts will be melted into His to flow as one.
- The treasures of this earth will fade away as we gaze into the light of His Glory!

This is the hour we've been waiting for! Come, wonderful, Jesus, come!

And do this, knowing the time, that now it is high time to awake out of sleep; for now our salvation is nearer than when we first believed. The night is far spent, the day is at hand. Therefore let us cast off the works of darkness, and let us put on the armor of light. Let us walk properly, as in the day, not in revelry and drunkenness, not in lewdness and lust, not in strife and envy. But put on the Lord Jesus Christ, and make no provision for the flesh, to fulfill its lusts.

ROMANS 13:11-14

To the glory of God, the Father!

Almighty God, Maker of heaven and earth, we are a grateful people for all of the wonders of salvation You have given us. Even when we were dead in our trespasses and sins, You truly have raised us up to sit with You in heavenly places in Christ Jesus so that You might show us the exceeding riches of Your grace throughout all ages!

May the eyes of our understanding be flooded with light from Your glorious Word that we may comprehend the mighty power You have so freely given. This same power that raised Christ Jesus from the dead has raised us up to walk in newness of life with You.

You have imparted Your righteousness into us by Your grace—a gift so wondrous, it must be painted on our hearts by the Spirit of the Living God!

Help us, dear Father, to count all things as loss that we might know Jesus Christ our Lord – that we might be found in Him, not having our own righteousness but the righteousness which is through faith in Him. We pray that we might know and experience the victorious power of His resurrection even while we live in this physical body. May it truly be said that in Him we live and move and have our being.

We are grateful for the precious Blood of the Lamb and the Cross of Calvary that redeemed and reconciled us unto Yourself. We are grateful You have wiped away our yesterdays to open the doors for bright tomorrows. To You, Father, belongs all the glory and praise for our great salvation! What an incredible love that we should be called the children of God. In the Name of our Lord, the Righteous Jesus Christ. Amen.

Today, I pray that you will be able to declare with the prophet Isaiah:

> *I will greatly rejoice in the Lord,*
> *My soul shall be joyful in my God;*
> *For He has clothed me with the*
> *garments of salvation,*
> *He has covered me with the*
> *robe of righteousness....*
> ISAIAH 61:10

For a Complete List of Books,
Tapes and Media Materials or to
Schedule the Author for Conferences,
Seminars and Speaking Engagements,
Contact:

Dr. Sandra G. Kennedy
Sandra Kennedy Ministries
2621 Washington Road
Augusta, GA 30904

Phone: 706-737-4530
Fax: 706-737-4113

Internet: www.sandrakenndey.org
www.wholelife.org
Email: wlm@wholelife.org